A Kind of Love Story

A Kind of Love Story

Tom Sellers

My restaurant is my home:

I work there.

Sweat there.

Bleed there.

Create there.

Sleep there.

And will most probably die there.

This book is about finding where you belong and pushing yourself to the limits.

It is for the believers, for all those people who dare to dream.

I believe in the power of food to tell a story, spark conversation, make people smile. Change lives.

The moment I fell in love with food it changed mine.

People sometimes say that food is an art form, and art's only purpose is to be itself. I think that's bollocks. Food is so much more than style or ingredients. It is about emotion and memories. It can be challenging and entertaining. It can take you to an exciting place.

A Kind of Love Story

I am nowhere near fully formed as a cook; I don't think anyone ever is.

We are all on a journey of discovery.

The way I cook and think about food won't be the same next year, as now.

Things move fast.

In five years' time I'll probably be using techniques and ingredients that none of us have even heard of yet. Because we have only discovered a fraction of what is out there.

There isn't a single full stop in the evolution of food. That is the beauty and excitement of it. Progress is the pulse of the kitchen. It's what keeps us alive.

There will always be more stories to tell and more people to tell them.

Cooking doesn't define me,
but the need to achieve does.
Am I obsessed with cooking?
Or is cooking the medium
I have chosen to feed my
obsession to learn, improve,
achieve? It's an interesting
question. I only know that
from the first time I set
foot in a kitchen I loved
everything about it: the heat,
the challenge, the pressure,
the potential for violence.
The kitchen is the only place
in which I have ever felt
I belonged.

1

Service

I still get that excited, nervous, anxious, butterfly feeling before every service starts, but I like this early evening time in the kitchen, when the music is on and the banter and the jokes are flying, while *6pm* everyone works, deftly, smoothly, calmly. We all know what is coming. In forty-five minutes it will be insane, full-on, total focus.

A bag of jelly babies is doing the rounds and is gone in moments; bottles of water and sugary drinks are being downed. Frank (FG), my sous chef, is plunging a can into liquid nitrogen to cool it down. Everyone needs sugar and hydration to keep going.

   – Table 5 is in the house . . .

   – Yes, Chef!

The guests are coming in, the snacks are going out. Quick hands are piping dots of smoked cod roe emulsion onto crispy cod skins then finishing them with sprigs of carrot tops. Radishes filled with kelp butter are sent out on folded napkins. The Pea Diddy, as we call it in the kitchen, is back on – a snack of fresh pea pods with peas and dots of black truffle purée inside.

The guy on Table 3 has just plucked a pink rose from the little garden outside the restaurant on his way in and presented it to the girl he is meeting for dinner. Cheeky. That's something I would probably do.

She is looking impressed; either because she didn't see, and she thinks he arrived with it. Or she likes his bravado.

From our glass box of a kitchen we see the guests and they see us. I want them to feel that we are enjoying ourselves as much as they are, because we love what we do.

We are a tight family: young, professional, slick, no passengers, everyone totally committed to giving their all, but we don't take ourselves too seriously.

It wasn't always this smooth. In the early days of Story every service was a crisis. We had five chefs and me. It was fucking insane, a blur. Everyone screaming at each other. Me trying to cook everything, touch everything, taste everything, because I hadn't learned how to take a step back; how to trust the people around me. At the end of the lunchtime service I used to fall asleep on the counter in the kitchen because I was so exhausted I couldn't move.

I don't think anything or anybody can totally prepare you for opening the doors of your first restaurant: spotlights on; show time. I remember the first night, seeing the first guests arriving and thinking, 'They are actually coming to eat *my* food.' It wasn't fear. It was excitement.

Legacy

I think the hardest thing for a chef is to establish your own identity in food, because of course you soak up influences everywhere you work. Doesn't everyone, in any walk of life? But inevitably once you open your own doors people will always make comparisons.

I embrace that, though. I have worked in some of the best restaurants in the world, with some of the greatest cooks that walk this planet, and they, in turn, have taken qualities from the great chefs they trained with. That is the way food evolves.

I don't want to shy away from any of those influences; I want to celebrate them, acknowledge them as a way of paying respect to the people who have taught me, showed me the way.

Ultimately I believe you have to take the best of every experience and then forge your own identity. Identity is what it is all about. There are a lot of great restaurants that produce beautiful dishes to perfection, but so many of them could have come out of the same box.

Potwash

I didn't set out to be a chef. But when you are sixteen, and there's a job going washing pots at a local pub, a few shifts a week, £5 an hour, that's enough to keep you in trainers and jeans. I was fast at washing pots, still am. I can put a dishwasher to shame – and I'm better for the environment!

The pub was the Hammer and Pincers near Nottingham and I had no idea what to expect. It was just a job. But straight away I was attracted to the environment of the kitchen. It reminded me of the building site where I did some stints labouring when I left school: proper hard work, digging trenches, laying pipes. Tough in winter, but nice in the summer; radio on, banter, fun, initiations, I loved all of that, and the physicality of it. I was very fit from all the sports that I played: ice hockey, martial arts, football. In the kitchen I sensed the same mix of boyish pranks, humour and sheer hard work, pushing through the pain barrier of being tired. Plus, even at that level, you had to work at pace, under pressure.

When I look back now I think if I had grown up wanting to be a chef because I loved food and cooking, then I never would have got to where I am today. Because the reality of working in a restaurant kitchen has nothing to do with romance. For a start you have to be able to stand on your feet for up to eighteen hours a day, five days in a row and physically take the heat, which, in some kitchens, means that the sweat is literally running off you in the height of summer. And in the winter, if the kitchen is downstairs, you barely see daylight, which can send you crazy at times.

But I had no expectations, and I was hooked. I could see that the kitchen becomes your home and everyone in it part of your family. You look after each other, have each other's backs, share the load, or sometimes there are clashes of personality, jealousies, power struggles, fights and flare-ups under pressure; stuff that happens in most families.

Perhaps it was fate that the head chef was Damian Clisby, who worked at places like Pied a Terre and with Mark Hix before becoming head chef at Petersham Nurseries. He was only at the Hammer and Pincers because he was going through a divorce and had moved to the country for a spell to clear his head.

He was a very good chef, systematic, astute, and he was producing really good food – everything done from scratch: fish, butchery, all the meat bones roasted for the pots of home-made stocks and sauces on the stove. For some reason Damian noticed me. He started handing me other things to do. One day he told me to go to the back fridge and get some chervil. I opened the fridge and there were a million green things in there – what the fuck was chervil? I just brought him every single herb I could see.

Over the weeks I started doing more and more shifts until I was working every day, and Damian started stepping up the tasks: potatoes to be sliced for dauphinoise, vegetables for a lamb dish, sweet paste for a lemon tart. Then he put a whole fish in front of me, and showed me how to fillet it. Good hand-eye co-ordination is essential for a chef and I discovered I was naturally dexterous.

It was hard work but we had fun. One Saturday night after service we went out on the town in Nottingham until the early hours when Damian realised he had locked himself out – he was living above the pub at the time – so I managed to break the latch on one of the kitchen windows that was slightly open and climb through. I remember I had a new top on and I ripped it on the latch. I let Damian in and we made steak sandwiches in the kitchen at about three in the morning, then he said, 'Right, see you back here at eight ready for Sunday lunch.' I loved all that. I guess it appealed to the naughty kid in me that used to ring people's doorbells and run away.

When Damian took a new job at Langar Hall, a country house hotel, I went too. I started working on the stoves with him. One day he said, 'Tom, you are naturally good at this. You need to bring in a notebook and write things down.'

The first thing I wrote in my book was how to make prawn stock. I had never thought about any kind of stock before, let alone one made from seafood. I had no idea it was even possible to roast the heads and shells of prawns in a pan and add water to make the most delicate liquid. How beautiful was that?

I learned that as a chef you had to develop and fine-tune your palate, to understand salt, acidity, sweet, sour, bitter. Bitter – what was that? It was a flavour I had never experienced. We didn't even have grapefruit at home. Oranges, apples, bananas, yes, but bitter wasn't on my radar.

The first thing I made from start to finish was tomato fondue. What a horrible job: skinning, de-seeding and chopping mounds and mounds of tomatoes, then sweating down the flesh until it was like a relish.

But I was falling in love with food. Sometimes I wonder which came first, my obsession to achieve, to prove all the doubters wrong, or my obsession with food. Whatever; they became the same thing. Everything else – hanging out with mates, girlfriends, playing sport – became irrelevant. I wanted to know everything, do everything. I couldn't stop asking questions. How do you do this? How does that work?

At school I had hated the confinement of the classroom. I just wanted to be free. I could see that there were rules in kitchens too, and certain foundations you needed to learn, but also I could see that cooking, like art or music, knows no boundaries. When I cooked it felt like pure escapism and that was the greatest feeling.

Yes, cooking is about control, but it is also about freedom. I don't see any paradox in that. If you have all freedom and no control, you have chaos and confusion; if you have all control and no freedom you have sterility and boredom.

Bring the two together and you can do anything you dare to dream about. I could walk into the kitchen at Story tomorrow and put anything I like on the menu. Who's to say whether I am right or wrong? The only question is whether you like it or not.

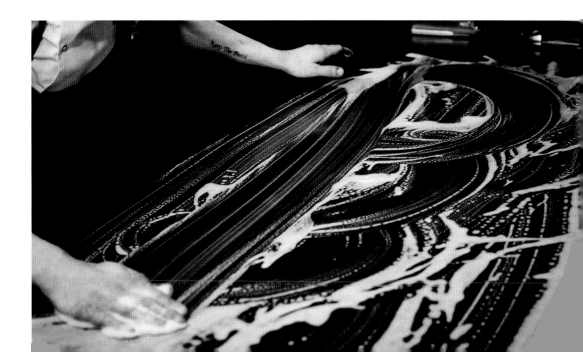

Trying = Success or Failure = Knowledge

Without knowledge, what is a recipe, but a set of instructions?

Follow a recipe blindly, and what do you learn?

Recipes can close you in and hold you back.

What truly counts is getting to know your ingredients; understanding how they work together.

5g of salt or a tablespoon of lemon juice in a recipe – *why?*

Understanding what salt or acidity does to food, opening your palate to flavours, and your mind to experimentation and the possibility of failure – all that equals knowledge, equals freedom.

The lesson people miss is that however long you have been cooking, at whatever level, you are learning every day, still getting things wrong, still discovering.

Sometimes you learn from brilliant mistakes.

All that happens over time is that as your fund of knowledge gets bigger, your window of failure hopefully gets smaller.

Through trying you succeed or fail, but either way you gain knowledge, and then use it to move on. That is how it works for me.

'Success is not final.
Failure is not fatal:
it is the courage
to continue that
counts.'

Winston Churchill (misquoted).
He probably never actually
said it but for me it encapsulates
everything I believe.

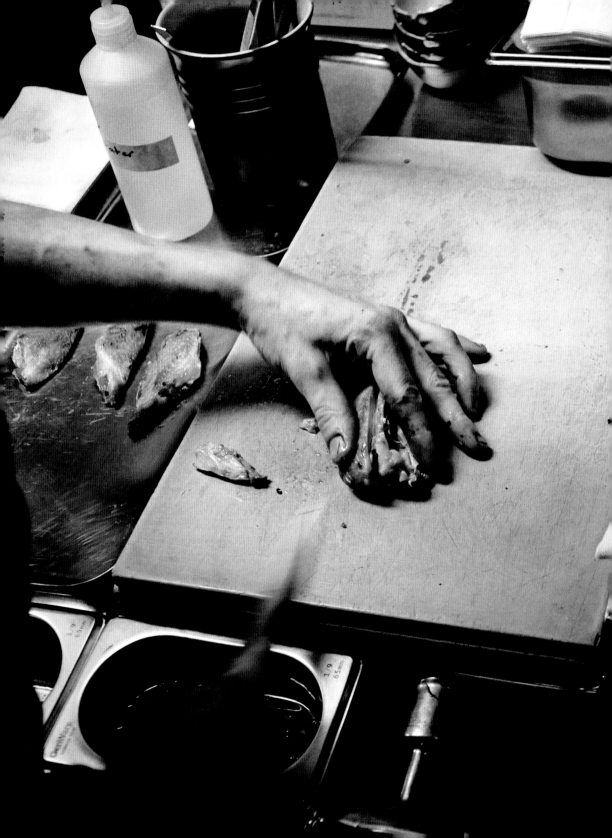

London

My mum was brushing her teeth in the bathroom, ready for bed, when I came home one night.

– Mum, I need to talk to you. I'm going to be a chef.

– What do you want to do that for? It's terrible hours, terrible money!

– Yeah, but I love food.

– You've only been working for a few weeks . . .

– Mum, I promise you, I love food.

At Langar Hall Damian talked about the kitchens he had worked in. One day he said, 'You should go and work in London.'

– Where should I go?

– Tom Aikens.

– Why?

– Because he's basically ten of me.

– OK.

I rang the restaurant, Tom Aikens. Said I would like to come for a trial.

It was 7 a.m. when I arrived, and pitch black outside. As I walked downstairs to the kitchen, the stoves were already roaring, chefs were sweating and Tom was shouting.

 – *Hi, I'm . . .*

 – *Here, dice this fennel.*

I was totally overwhelmed but excited by everything: the detail and the complexity of the food, the huge amount of pressure that everyone seemed to be working under. All day it was do this, get that . . . these guys were doing things with food that I didn't think possible. It was a universe away from rump of lamb and vegetables at Langar Hall. But at the end of the day Tom said, 'There's a job going if you want it. Twelve grand a year. Start tomorrow. 6 a.m.'

OK. Wow.

Three weeks later I realised: of course there was a job. Chefs were leaving at the rate of about one a week. Tom's was the hardest kitchen in London.

Spoon

Taste it; taste it! Grab a spoon. Hurry up and taste it . . .

Flavours develop and change all the time: too sharp, too salty, too sweet, too bland. You have to boss it all the time: and your most important tool? A spoon.

In the last ten years of my life I have had a spoon in my hand or tucked into a pocket of my apron for about eighteen hours a day. A spoon is the bridge between a chef and his work. Some of my proudest moments have been thanks to a little piece of metal.

I can get pretty worked up over spoons.

A knife is aggressive, a fork is a vehicle, but the spoon is everything: welcoming, rounded, nothing about it sharp or dangerous.

The first time a spoon went into your mouth, chances are it was your mother, father or a loved one who was holding it, forming your earliest food memories, your likes and dislikes, giving you soothing things like soup, treats like ice cream, caring things like medicine.

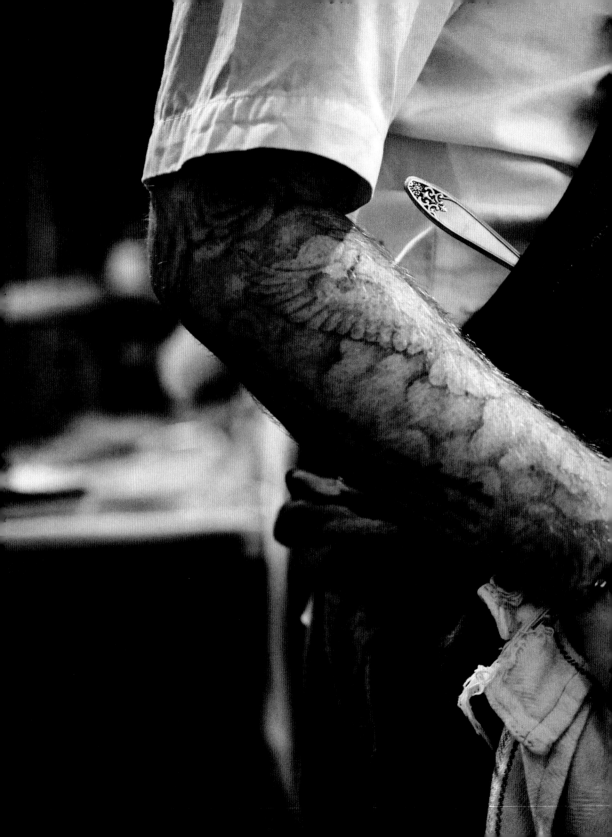

Service

— FG, I need five bad-ass langoustines, live and kicking tomorrow.

FG is controlling the prep kitchen downstairs, checking fridges, asking the boys what they need, placing orders for the next day.

At 6.30 p.m. he comes up and joins in with service on the cold side.

Angelo, my head chef, is running the service. His role is to have a grander sense of everything that is happening; he knows exactly what stage every table is at. Between us we are holding a huge amount of information in our heads at any one time. Twenty-one snacks and dishes to every table; a person on Table 2 doesn't eat fish; someone on Table 5 is allergic to gluten . . . As the night goes on he becomes more and more drawn to the hot side of the kitchen, dressing the plates. Swift, dexterous.

Angelo is creative, he has a great eye and speed and gentleness in his hands. Everything about the way he moves in the kitchen has finesse. There is so much soul in his food. But he also has drive, needs to be continuously challenged. He reminds me of me, when I was working for Tom Aikens. And when he finds his own true identity he can be better than me. I have no shame in saying that.

But you can't have a team full of flair players, you

also have to have the guy who plays the sweeper role, holds up the ball, knows the club inside out, has an aura about him in the dressing room. FG is that man.

FG is the opposite of me. It takes a lot to ruffle him. He hates any confrontation; he likes to settle things with logic and humour. And he has a great palate. I joke with him that that's because he went to school at Marlborough College, so he was probably eating caviar when he was six.

FG has been here since the beginning, and I was fiercely hard on him at times, irrational in the early days.

At our lowest point, I completely lost it when he left the fridge door open. How ridiculous is that! It was a measure of the stress we were all under. I told him to get the fuck out. He refused to leave. Thank God for me he understood that everything was coming from raw passion and pressure.

FG is someone who totally understands and adores food, but right now he is feeling divorced from cooking because I have got him talking to farmers, foragers, fishermen, dealing with logistics.

I understand exactly how he feels. When you are a cook you never want to have to deal with the reality of management.

But he will thank me one day, when he wants to open a restaurant of his own. To be able to pick up the phone to a vegetable supplier you know on a personal basis, and say, 'I'm opening my own place, can you supply me?' is invaluable. I know because I've been there. Not just suppliers, but people who have been vital to Story, like Rod, who built my kitchen, and David Ball, the designer who created our menus and our website – our relationships were forged way back when I worked with Tom Aikens.

But I hope all that is a long way down the line, because the biggest compliment I can pay FG is that I genuinely can't imagine this restaurant without him.

FG, Angelo, me, the three of us are very close. We've been through a lot together. They must fucking hate me at times!

To be the best, you have to sign the best, because the good guys are hard to find and hang onto. Bigger restaurants can pay better than me in the transfer market.

  – *Table 8 is in the house.*

Lettuce is charring on the barbeque.

Rabbit sandwiches are lined up like little soldiers.

Plates are ready at different temperatures. Some in the fridge, some briefly in the freezer. I am very particular about all of that. It's all about the guest eating the food at the right temperature.

All our plates are different, hand-made. I saw a woman casually put one in her handbag one night! So many people turned me away, said our project wasn't big enough. I was beginning to lose faith, but then I saw Lok Ming Fung's beautiful ceramics, and fortunately for us she decided to buy the ticket and jump on board the bus with us.

The dining room is filling up and chefs and waiters take it in turns to take the food to the tables, explain it to the guests. It's not a natural role for a chef, but it's all part of breaking down the barriers between the kitchen and the guest. You can see that some of the guys are more comfortable than others. FG is brilliant at it.

Everyone loves a guest who is enthusiastic, interested,

questioning. But you can't expect it all the time. You might have a couple so wrapped up in each other, you could be standing there with no clothes on, and they wouldn't notice.

When it starts to get dark the whole atmosphere in the restaurant changes. I love that. How lucky am I to have a restaurant bang in the middle of London, looking out at the Shard all lit up every night.

Tomorrow is Friday, the hardest day. These boys are as tough as the marines. Maybe not physically, but mentally. But by Friday you've got a week of being on your feet since 6 a.m. stacking up behind you. That's when tiredness, impatience and frustration can come through.

When Saturday comes you can get through anything. It wouldn't matter if the stove fell apart, because on Sunday you can sleep.

'I remember walking away from our first meeting on a rainy winter's day in 2012, feeling the buzz, and excited to be involved in the Story project. When I first met Tom, I could see the passion he had for cooking and food, but equally he saw the importance of a unique and handcrafted plate.'

Lok Ming Fung,
ceramics designer

Nottingham

People often say to me, 'I could never have stuck the pressure or the hours you had to work in Tom's kitchen at such a young age,' but actually, if you grew up where I did, you probably could.

The two most important elements that shape your life are the ones over which you have no control: who your parents are and where you were born and raised.

Everything about the way I was brought up taught me never to give up or give in.

The neighbourhood in Nottingham was, and is, tough. It's a tough city, and it breeds hard characters. There were places you wouldn't walk after nine o'clock at night, and sometimes busloads of lads from the different estates would come down looking for a fight; the further the estate was towards the inner city the harder and more dangerous the gangs. Did falling in love with food and with cooking save me from a very different life? Maybe. Was I looking for an escape? Probably.

From an early age my dad taught me and my brother Oliver to look after ourselves, stand our ground and most importantly stand up for each other and for my sister. 'Never leave your brother. Two are stronger than one.' So as kids we always had each other's backs.

My dad is a man's man, a welder by trade with hands

the size of teapots, and he is my hero. A strong, proud, man who had the toughest of upbringings and showed me that you get nothing out of life unless you work hard for it. To me he is the kindest, most generous man. Dad was old-school, mind. His mantra was that if you had a problem with someone you sorted it out with your bare hands – step outside into a field or the car park and deal with it like men. Sometimes you'd even shake hands afterwards; but more often the animosity would burn on down through the generations. Trouble would have a way of finding us. There would always be some guy in the pub who'd had one too many beers and wanted to take us on.

Oliver and I have the same fiery blood in our veins. We are exactly a year bar a day apart and I am the oldest. At school we were a handful, always in trouble, sneaking out of lessons, pea-shooting the teacher, smashing windows. You name it, we did it. Stupid, stupid stuff. I was suspended three times; always for fighting. I had my nose broken and my thumb, cracked a few teeth, needed loads of stitches. My brother and I left school with the reputation that you didn't mess with the Sellers boys. Go after Oliver, and Thomas would come after you and vice versa.

My mum spent a lot of her time worried and upset. The teachers used to say to her, 'Tom is really bright but he just doesn't come to school to work.' I treated the place like a youth club; but I still couldn't wait to get out at the end of the day. 'Have you done your homework, Tom?' 'No.' 'Stand outside in detention.' That was how it went.

The funny thing is, somehow, sitting in the classroom, wherever my mind was, something was sinking in. I never studied for a single GCSE, but I got decent grades in almost all of them. I remember sitting in the English Literature exam and writing about pathetic fallacy in *Lord of the Flies*. Hand on heart I never studied the book. My English teacher saw the paper and said to me, 'Tom, how did you do that?!' 'You talked about it one day, Miss.' 'But you were never listening!' Clearly I was.

The only GCSE I failed was what they used to call Home Economics: cooking! I never took it seriously. What was I going to do with an egg? Throw it obviously!

There were reasons why my dad was at war with the world when he was younger, and why he was so determined that my brother and I would grow up able to look out for ourselves and each other. He came from a very poor family; I mean, really poor. He was one of nine, with seven sisters and a brother, and they were brought up very strictly with no money for any luxuries. My dad used to say they had one fry-up a year and that was on Christmas morning. But then his father died when he was about twelve, and his mother didn't know how to cope. My dad went off the rails and became uncontrollable at school, so when he was fifteen he was sent to borstal – one of those old-school detention centres run by the prison service for so-called young 'delinquents' that were abolished in the eighties. Fifteen! It was really unusual for anyone so young to be sent there, and it was so tough that he escaped three times. Once he hid in a loft belonging to one of his older married sisters for two days until they found him and took him back.

I don't remember many father-son chats when I was growing up. Even now we don't find it easy to talk to each other on an emotional level, and I only saw my dad cry twice. Once when my sister had pneumonia when we were kids and ended up in intensive care, and once when we went out and had a few drinks too many and he told me some of the things that happened to him in borstal. Fucked-up stuff. There were two brothers especially who bullied him, and a lot of the time he was petrified. Even after all this time, I could see the hurt and anger in his eyes when he talked about it. He has tattoos on his fingers that he did himself when he was in there, and although he hasn't said so, I think he was made to do them. So when he came out he was hardened, and if someone taunted him or crossed him he would lash out.

My mum played a big part in changing his life, I think, and in comparison to his own childhood me and my brother and sister grew up like millionaires, because both my mum and dad worked so hard to look after us. We always had nice food on the table, a car, holidays.

My dad is who he is, and I love him for all of it. He made me strong. Any time I have been in a situation where I've felt like giving up, I would always think, 'What would Dad say?' And carry on.

I wouldn't change my upbringing for the world. My parents are the best; and I would give them everything. I always used to tell my mum, 'I want to make you proud,' and she would say, 'We are already proud. We love you.'

– *But I want to make you proud proud.*

'*Tom is super-smart at managing people. If someone does something wrong, he'll let his anger out, but two minutes later, he'll make it up with them, which stops any doubts or anger or resentment building up. Then it's like nothing happened.*'

Angelo,
head chef

Sunday Dinner

What a beautiful thing Sunday dinner is. Food is about so much more than ingredients, recipes, technique or training. It's about emotion, the setting and the context, the mood you are in, who you are with, the associations with memory. It's a powerful thing.

As a family we always ate Sunday dinner, usually in the late afternoon: a rump of beef or chicken, roast potatoes, cauliflower cheese . . . Mum would put the joint in and then we would go to the local pub. Dad would be going up to the bar for his third pint:

– *The roast is going to be ready, George.*

– *We've just got time for one more.*

When we got home it would be, 'Megan, lay the table', 'Oliver, sort out the drinks', 'Thomas, help me with the potatoes'. Just for one day, everyone came together around the dinner table. I loved it.

My mum worked full-time, but she still cooked every day, nothing out of the ordinary (though she'll call me a cheeky bugger for saying so), just good family food: she made a mean lasagne, or there would be cottage pie, sometimes fish fingers, chips and beans. The Friday treat was a jacket potato, because Mum would let you choose the filling: whatever you wanted.

If I am honest, though, when I was growing up I don't know that I ever appreciated food being much more than fuel to keep you going. Every day was hectic in our house. My brother and I played sport and my sister used to ride and dance after school, so when we came in Mum just wanted us to sit down and be still around the dinner table – even for half an hour. She would get so upset if the food was ready and we were nowhere to be seen, or my brother and I wanted to eat in front of the TV because there was football on.

Even if Mum gave in to us she would always eat her own meal at the table, sometimes all by herself. I think about that a lot now, about how, even when she was so busy, she put in the time to cook for everyone, and we didn't understand or appreciate the love that involved, and the importance of taking time to enjoy it all together. Except on Sundays. Sunday dinner was different.

BURNT ONIONS, APPLE & GIN

The most exciting week of the year for our family was when the fair came to Loughborough nearby – it was the biggest street fair in Europe and me and my brother and sister could hardly wait until my dad came home from work. It would be cold, and we would get all wrapped up. I'd be on my dad's shoulders and what I remember most vividly when we were walking around was the smell of the onions cooking for the hot dogs. It makes me happy just thinking about it now. So that's what got me into making a dish all about onions. In most kitchens and most cuisines, onions are a stage-builder, a base layer or a great number two: beef and onion, cheese and onion . . . but I wanted the onion to be the whole story. Take an onion, and make it amazing.

Gin is something I fell in love with later. When you first have an alcoholic drink, I don't think you actually like drinking. You don't really like the taste of beer as a teenager. Or wine, or spirits. Then slowly, you start to understand, and gin is the first drink I really got to know.

My mum always says that when my dad drinks gin he becomes all soft and loving and mushy, so I thought that onions plus gin would make for a very happy plate of food: my nostalgic childhood memory married with my adult alcohol of choice.

It began with the emotion and the narrative, but once I started turning over the idea in my brain, I felt

it could work because of the juniper and the botanicals in the gin. We tested lots of different gins and
eventually we decided on Jensen's Old Tom, not just
for the name and the style, but for the story behind
it. Old Tom gin first appeared in the early nineteenth
century, at a crossover time when the poorer people
of London were still getting drunk in the gin palaces,
but gin cocktails were also becoming the fashion if
you were rich and glamorous. The gin tended to be
sweetened, either by the distiller, or in the drinking
palaces, where sugar was often added.

Vintage gin maker Christian Jensen first started
making Old Tom in small batches to a handwritten – but unsweetened – recipe that he found in a
distiller's notebook, dating from the 1840s. Since
it is designed as a cocktail gin, it has the perfect
balance of botanicals that we need to work with the
flavours of green apple and lemon thyme, because we
use the alcohol in quite a raw way. The opposite to
using wine in a casserole, in which you burn off the
alcohol and then let it cook slowly in the sauce to
give it richness.

I could never use Monkey 47, for example, which is
my ultimate gin to drink, because it is named after
the fact that it has forty-seven botanicals in it, even
cranberry. That is way too complex and floral.

So the dish is all about onions, but done in four
ways. We use pink Roscoff onions, which are sweeter
than most, and also have a whole story of their own.
They're the ones that, in the first part of the twen-
tieth century, Frenchmen wearing berets, known as
'johnnies', used to bring over to Plymouth by boat
from Roscoff. Then they would peddle around the
country on their bikes with the strings of the onions
hung all over their handlebars, selling them door
to door.

We leave the skin of the onions on, to trap in the
moisture, cut them in half and sauté them hard, cut-

side down in a hot pan, because I want them to burn and blacken around the edges like fairground onions, but still stay a little bit 'rare', because we want a bit of rawness and texture. Everyone loves that hint of raw onion, don't they? Think of cheese with raw onion – another memory from the food bank. When the onions have blackened, we add some sea salt – only now, as salt draws out moisture – and butter, then take off the skin and root and separate the layers into shells. They sit on mounds of classic Lyonnaise-style onions that we have thinly sliced and cooked over a long period of time, to bring out their natural sugars.

Into the shells go some onions we have pickled in beer, then we add an onion crisp and, depending on the time of year, some chickweed, maybe fat hen, or ramsons (wild garlic) and their flowers.

The sweetness of the onions needs to be balanced with acidity, which comes from Granny Smith apples. We juice them, make a warm apple consommé then add the gin, so the residual heat just takes the edge off the alcohol. Finally we add the floral, emerald green lemon thyme oil. The thyme is blanched, dried and spun in the Thermomix: 7-7-7. Speed seven, seven minutes at seventy degrees. The colour marries with the green apple – and the waiter pours it over the onions at the table.

That sauce is what brings everything together: the heat, warmth and burnt sweetness from the onions, the natural sharpness and acidity of the apple, the rawness of the gin, and the flowery flavour of the thyme.

Think of it like throwing a silk robe over the top, which falls and settles softly into all the cracks and crevices – it not only coats the ingredients but it coats your palate too and lingers on in the mouth.

Friday

I can't sleep. When I can't sleep I pace around, try to watch TV, but nothing works. I can't sleep because I am looking at last night's data report. It tells me how many guests were in the restaurant, what they ate, how much they spent, whether the service went smoothly, except I know it is incorrect. The number of guests is wrong and there are no notes. The restaurant was closed last night with just the basics inputted, and it annoys me. I hate a lack of attention and focus. If we are going to do the thing, we do it properly, or there's no point.

4 a.m.

By 6 a.m. I've slept for maybe two hours. I wake up to emails from my agent, Borra, and a supplier saying we have an overdue account – how can that be true? I make a mental note to investigate.

Breakfast meeting with my business partner Bob Leckie and shareholders.

7 a.m.

We've seen an amazing building nearby that could be a great cocktail bar, with a small menu, but the news is negative. The owner is dragging his feet over the sale.

The accountant is talking numbers and year-end figures and I am nodding, but what is running through my head is that Raymond Blanc is coming in for lunch tomorrow and we have two new dishes on the menu. And in three days' time we have a dinner table of seven chefs with a combined total of twelve Michelin stars between them. These are huge moments for all of the team, the days you dream about and dread at the same time: cooking for heroes.

There are times when it still seems unreal to me that Bob pledged so much money to Story on the strength of my word. I sat across the table from this complete stranger, who asked me what I wanted to do with this site that used to be a public toilet block in the middle of the road near London Bridge. I said, 'Make it the best restaurant in London if not the world.' And he believed in me. So much so that he never even ate my food until the opening night. How fucking crazy is that? What a fantastic guy.

But when business meets food, you've just opened a new door as a cook. One that involves a lot of money, a lot of risk. All of a sudden you are answerable to shareholders and backers and accountants. When I dreamed about my own restaurant never once did I hear someone saying, 'OK, Tom, you can do this, or that, but this month we will lose money.' The business side has no romance, no love. Everything is a huge decision. If I want to put turbot on the menu instead of cod it's a big financial issue. If I want to try to get a second Michelin star, do I need two sommeliers instead of one? Do I need someone to stand permanently on the door? Huge decisions.

I've always seen compromise as failure, believed you have to risk everything to achieve something great, but I've had to find maturity pretty quickly and be big enough to listen to the people that are saying no, because you can only have a restaurant if it stays open. My job is to be the visionary, to focus on being better every day, and to fill the dining room with people who want to eat great food and be entertained, but some trade-offs you have to make; and some days I feel massively under pressure.

'He wants to be a winner,
all the time.
Honest, single-minded,
calls a spade a spade,
I know he has the
determination to get to
where he wants to be.' Bob Leckie,
business partner

At least the tea and poached egg on toast are perfect and I feel better going to the restaurant with a fuelled body.

The kitchen is already in full swing when I arrive from my meeting with my business partner. FG grabs me the moment I walk through the door. There is a leak and he can't reach the maintenance team. I change into my whites and make a call to them at the same time. All I get is the message machine.

In the kitchen, I go around everyone individually, as always, and say good morning. Ten chefs working at a hundred miles an hour; but there should be eleven.

7.45 a.m.

— *Where's Jack?*

— *Not here yet, Chef.*

— *What, he's fucking late again?*

— *Yes, Chef.*

— *Well, call him and get him out of fucking bed!*

Jack is our youngest apprentice and still getting to grips with the brutal hours this job demands. When I was his age I was working for Thomas Keller in America and I'd already been cooking for four years, but I remind myself I am not the norm; not many people have done it my way.

Some detective work tells me Jack was out at a party all night. Let's say I am not best impressed, but I'm going to cut him a bit of slack. I like him, he's a good kid, he is talented, intelligent, works hard and he definitely could go on and make his mark. I see in him someone who really cares. But he made a bad decision.

He finally shows up at 1 p.m., I take him to one side.

– *Why are you late, Jack?*

– *I went out last night and had too much to drink, Chef.*

I respect the fact that he told the truth. He could have given some bullshit about being ill, and I can see he is disappointed in himself. He is twenty-years-old, and he wants to go out and get pissed with his mates. I get it. But the other ten cooks in his restaurant family have had to pick up the slack and cover for him, all because he was irresponsible and didn't come into work. He has a duty to them and I tell him he has to make a lifestyle choice. 'Either you are one hundred per cent dedicated to your craft, or you can't be at Story.' He goes back into the kitchen and works with a fury.

CANDLE

I'm the candle-maker; a hundred candles a day.

The candle was the first dish I made as an independent cook and it encapsulates everything I feel about the power of food to tell a story.

Of all the narratives behind the dishes this is a bit of a dark one. It's about the love I never properly showed to my dad when I was growing up, in those times when our relationship drifted and occasionally collided when I was a teenager and behaved like teenagers do. Packed my bags and went to live with a friend once, until Mum pulled me back and knocked our heads together. And it's about proving to him, still, that I have the will and dedication to work hard and succeed.

Bread and dripping is so British and working class and my dad loves it, used to eat it every Sunday when I was a kid – proper dripping from the leftover fats and meat juices and jelly from the Sunday roast. But I never liked it then.

Everyone on the floor knows that the candle is inspired by my dad's love of bread and dripping, but I've never told him it signifies anything more. That sums us up. We don't have many deep conversations. But he always taught me: 'no matter where you are in the world, never forget who you are and where you come from.'

All the time I was thinking about my own restaurant and what I would put on the menu, I wanted bread and dripping. The idea had been playing in my mind for a while, then one day I was watching wax run down the side of a candle, and I thought, 'What if I set the dripping in the shape of a candle, would it melt in the same way? After all, before people made candles from wax they used animal tallow.'

So back home I started drawing pictures in my notebook and playing around in my mum's kitchen. She came home one day to find me and my dad and a load of beef fat and wicks everywhere. 'Tom, what *are* you doing?'

I'd spend ten hours a day rendering the fat at different temperatures. I discovered it was crucial that it was done very slowly at the right temperature. If it boiled, it would be too liquid and it would turn a dark colour instead of white and it would split as it set. If it was too cool it wouldn't set properly. Finally I settled on about twenty hours of slow rendering at eighty degrees.

I tried thin wicks and fat wicks that burned at different speeds. Then I had to find a way to keep the wick straight down the middle of the fat using a matchstick. If it isn't dead centre it won't burn properly.

Eventually my dad made the moulds for the candles, and the stands that hold them while they are setting, which we still use in the kitchen. I love the fact that he was so closely involved with the evolution of the dish, and when he eats it in the restaurant he is massively proud.

When Story was being built, I was interviewing chefs in my usual space in the coffee shop nearby. On this particular day I was interviewing Fran, who became my pastry chef for the opening of the restaurant. I was explaining the idea of the candle to her, what it

'Please may we have dripping toast, with the meat jelly underneath and a glass jug full of celery to crunch with it, as Flora Thompson used to eat (read Lark Rise), and we did too, when I was a child in Devon.

Also with bronzed watercress. Thank you!'

represented, how I wanted it to burn at the table for our guests, so that they could dip chunks of home-made bread into it. We had sourced old-fashioned Charles Dickens chamber candlesticks, all different, all original, from antique markets and flea markets to add another historical layer to the narrative.

It was an anxious time for me; I was taking big risks, and this dish was one of them. Would paying guests want to eat bread and dripping? Would they understand it? Would they love it or hate it?

As we were talking an elderly lady came over to the table. She told me she couldn't help overhearing my story, that it had reminded her of her childhood, and she handed me a piece of lined paper, torn from a notebook, on which she had written the words on the left. 'Make sure you read this,' she said, and then she left.

It was the most romantic moment for me. Like a scene from a movie. A chance encounter with a stranger left me feeling happy and confident that, yes, I was on the right track. I really could affect people with the narrative power of food.

And when I read what she had written, I understood that the bread and dripping needed something more, some meat jelly to give it depth, and something fresh and crunchy to cut through the fattiness. That little piece of paper was the inspiration for the relish that we served on the side, made with slow-cooked veal tongue, pickled horseradish, celery, parsley stems, rapeseed oil – and initially chicken jelly. Each element contributed something in terms of taste and texture: the tongue was quite soft, the jelly almost bouncy. You got the crunch of the parsley stems, acidity from the pickled horseradish, and then the rapeseed oil was the blanket of love that brought everything together.

The plan was always to replace the chicken jelly with the meat extract that separates from the fat during the process of rendering the meaty beef bones. But we had to wait. It was a year-long project collecting and preserving enough of that extract. Some things you just can't rush. When the first batch was finally ready we re-designed the relish, taking out the chicken jelly, and adding salted, diced celeriac instead, and now we serve a little pot of the soft jelly-like extract separately at room temperature. It is super-intense, beefy, Bovrilly, and full of umami.

Before the candles leave the kitchen we scatter some sea salt in the base of each holder and then start the dripping burning at the base of the candle with a blowtorch, so it begins to melt and form a pool. Then the waiter lights the wick at the table. In essence it is a very simple thing, but it is a little piece of theatre, a talking point, and it will always be special and personal to me; a symbol of hard work, dedication, the will to succeed.

I smile when I hear guests discussing it, swapping their own memories of bread and dripping, and I still have the piece of paper that special lady gave me. I often wonder if one day she will come into the restaurant.

Every review of Story I
read says I am twenty-six,
so I like to think I'll be
twenty-six forever.

Childhood

I think a lot of the playfulness and escapism that is in my food is sparked by childhood things. By my wanting to stay forever a child.

If I could be Peter Pan I would be.

I loved being a child, loved the freedom of the age between about seven and twelve, before people try to make you say what you want to be when you are older.

Maybe that is why I pushed so hard against school, because schools want you to grow up. I hated the regulation, the restriction of the classroom.

At weekends and on school holidays me and my brother would go out for the day and play in the fields and get totally lost in our imaginations, making up adventures, building tree houses and making dens from hay bales, or trying to stack them as high as we could, and getting chased by the farmer, always.

Or we'd run off with the bottles that the milkman delivered to doorsteps from his old float. We ran the game like a military operation. We had stash-holes in alleyways all around the neighbourhood. We knew all the houses that had orange juice delivered as well as milk: a bottle of juice scored more highly than milk – and some houses ordered yoghurt, too: that really was the money!

Evolution

The food that goes to the dining room has to aspire to be perfect, and it's rare to get a dish right first time, so the creative process can be long and hard behind the scenes. I live in two worlds: one of stories and romance, and one of logistics. In the middle is the restaurant, where I have to make both worlds meet and work.

Phase one. The narrative. A new dish begins in my head. I can taste it in my mind. I'll play around with it, draw it in my notebook, and come up with a handful of ingredients I want in that plate of food. Then I'll talk about it with FG and Angelo. My annoying line is always, 'I've tasted it in my dreams. Many times.'

Phase two. The key ingredients: how to treat them and how to bring them together. A plate of food can never be style over substance. It doesn't matter how romantic the story, or how good a dish looks, if it doesn't deliver flavour and integrity on every level, it's a failure.

Of course, what is in season together often works together. It's not coincidence. It's a message from nature. You could go out into the Kent countryside any day in autumn and pick apples, blackberries and cobnuts and make a stunning cobbler or crumble. Think about tomatoes and strawberries in summer – an unusual combination? Actually I think they can work together. They grow in the same habitat. They both love the sun. They turn from green to red. They're like brothers from different mothers. Together they give you acidity, sweetness, texture from the tomato, a little floral note. Maybe marry them with a little marjoram, thyme? Sage could work. Or go down the anise route: sweet cicely or chervil.

However secure you are in your combination of ingredients you have to find the right platform for them. Think about a classic duo like oysters and beef. If I poached the oysters in beef gravy, folded them through diced beef and kidneys and put them in a pie, that delicious saltiness of the sea working with the richness of the beef would be amazing. But if I decided it would be clever to make an oyster ice cream and put it on top of a piece of roast beef, that seriously wouldn't be nice.

When I think about the key ingredient I always ask myself: how has it grown up and where? In the ocean, on a tree, in the ground. . . what was its environment, what is its season? We research everything we can about it and then try to treat it in a familiar way.

In a way I find vegetables the easiest to understand. Think about a root vegetable growing underground without the gift of sunlight, that has never come in direct contact with the rain. Why would you throw it into water, an environment it has never been in before? The way my brain works, it makes sense to cook a root vegetable in a more robust, moody way: to bake it or roast it.

But if you take young fresh beans, or peas or asparagus that grow out in the sunlight, with the rain on their faces, they are at home with liquid. I don't want to roast or bake them, or braise them, I want their lightness and brightness to shine. So I would blanch, pickle or cook them really quickly, to capture their tenderness and freshness. The less you manipulate them, the better.

'Every ingredient that comes into the kitchen is seen as prestigious, to be cared for, treated like gold. With finesse. That is a massive word at Story: finesse.'

Liam, chef

Once we have our ingredients the real work in the kitchen begins, which is the revealing moment: you can be a few steps from the idea you imagined, or what feels like a million miles away. You might scribble out fifty per cent of the first draft, then whittle away at it until you make it work.

At this level it's a given that you can produce food that is technically at the highest level; the challenge is putting everything together, achieving the right balance of textures and flavours to create a dish that is more than the sum of its parts.

I don't put things on a plate because they look beautiful. I don't think, 'These flowers or these leaves or these stems look really attractive this month, so let's use them to dress a dish.' Fuck that, the way I think is: let's take all of the stems we can find in the whole of the UK and make a dish around them that changes through the seasons, but that is totally dependent on what tastes good. It starts and ends with taste: building layer on layer of flavour so that, as you eat, each component of the dish impacts on the one below.

You have to question the validity of every ingredient: what is it there for, what is a herb or a spice bringing to the dish? If it doesn't have a purpose it shouldn't be there.

What happens if you apply flame, smoke, steam, or cold?

Raw or cooked? In essence that should be one of the simpler choices. Actually it is one of the hardest. I still find it a challenge.

Is a carrot or a scallop better raw or cooked? Or just different?

Or beetroot? Very thinly sliced, raw, dressed with oil and salt. Wonderful. But bake it whole for three

hours enclosed in tin foil and it turns toffeeish, moreishly delicious.

If an exotic fruit has grown up in the most amazing tropical sunshine, where no one has tampered with it, then maybe you should do nothing at all with it. Take a ripe mango and just eat it like it is. Respect.

Hot and cold. There's something great about eating hot pudding with cold ice cream.

Sweet and sour.

Experiment.

Every time we go on the journey of a new dish it is a massive learning curve for all of us.

I'm not scared to fail.

The biggest lesson I have learned since opening Story is that it is hard to say 'stop'. It's a chef's nature to constantly think, 'I can make it better,' and since there are no rules, the possible results are endless. New young chefs are always tempted to add another texture, another sauce, a purée, a foam, three more flowers . . . But to say: 'I'm going to take three key elements, and stop'; to restrict yourself and pare things right back, you actually force yourself to be more creative.

It's the equivalent of setting out to build a vessel that can travel the ocean and having a yard full of every type of material and tool at your disposal, or being courageous enough to restrict yourself to three planks of wood and some string. Then you have to make sure that the result is fucking good. Simplicity has no safety net.

Angelo and I will work on the dish on a Sunday and Monday when the restaurant is closed and when I am happy, ultimately I just put it on a plate. Maybe

A cook who is afraid will often try too hard. In the wrong places.

In the end the journey of every dish is all about balance. Balancing emotion and narrative with research and technical know-how, to create something that tastes great.

my brain works naturally in quite an artistic way, but I don't spend hours designing how it is going to look. It seems to come easily.

Only when we are happy with the flavour, the texture, and, yes, of course the presentation, will we sit down with the whole team. Then it becomes a discussion with everyone.

Phase three. Logistics. Creating dreams and being able to make them a reality are two different things. How you orchestrate the kitchen, balance the workload and have every component of a dish come together in harmony at the right time to go out to the dining room is a crucial skill in itself. Every new dish impacts on the rhythm of the kitchen, and who does what, when.

I have to constantly put myself in the position of a chef de partie, and ask myself: is what I am asking actually possible in a tight team like ours? Every aspect has to come into play: how many chefs you have, the time a process will take, the space it needs. You have to spread the load between the hot and cold side of the kitchen. If a senior member of staff says to me, 'Chef, this won't work,' I listen.

We approach things like a Formula One team over a Grand Prix weekend: practice, qualifying and race day. Practice involves endless man-hours with the relevant chefs road-testing every single component of a dish, until everyone is happy. Qualifying involves a dry run during service, when we will make the dish under pressure, but not serve it to the guests. It's all about being systematic, minimising risks.

Race day is show time. You have done everything you can to be ready, but you have to be aware that the unexpected can happen, and inevitably the ride won't be one hundred per cent smooth.

Service

I see people coming in straight from work, often they are stressed, maybe they are running a little late and their partner or friends are sitting there waiting for them.

Ten minutes later when they have been given their eighth snack, I can see them unwinding, engaging with the story, in the bubble.

I see everything; hear everything. Ask the boys. It drives them crazy sometimes, because I never miss anything that happens in the kitchen or the dining room.

I'm the conductor. My role is to bring the volume and tone up or down in the kitchen or on the floor as I think necessary. If there's not enough energy or people aren't focused enough, it's unlucky for the next guy to make a mistake, because they'll get a bollocking, which sends a message to everyone. I hate that we can have a bad service just because people aren't switched on from kick-off, then all of a sudden the kitchen is behind and everyone is on the back foot.

But equally, if I need to turn things down, if the pressure is getting too intense, I'll go off-piste and make them laugh or go to the downstairs kitchen and talk about football with the boys for five minutes.

When Story was being built the one thing I was sure

of was that I wanted the main kitchen to be on the same floor as the dining room – comforting, as if you were at home – and I wanted the guests to be able to see in, and the chefs to see out.

It was one of the first business battles I had to win . . . 'But Tom, it means losing twenty seats . . .'

Otherwise, a plate of food arrives at your table, and you might think, 'Oh, that looks pretty,' and eat and enjoy it, but you make no connection with the people who have produced it.

At my most romantic I'd like to think that when guests sit down at the table it's a bit like going to the cinema and watching the trailers: half a dozen movies with all the action just glimpsed, so you think, 'I really want to see that!' That's what you get through the glass box of the kitchen: a flash of a flame from the Green Egg barbecue, a glimpse of action and banter.

Then when the food starts to arrive I want people to engage with us, be entertained, involved. That's where the knowledge that the waiters bring to the table comes in. If you understand something, I believe you will enjoy it more. Of course food is subjective, and we know we can't please everyone; not everyone will like everything or understand what we are trying to do. Some dishes always divide opinion. But if we can touch people's emotions, and spark a conversation, get a debate going, that's exciting. Like watching a challenging film. Take *American Beauty* – you might think, 'I don't really get it,' but then you talk about it with friends and if you do get it, you think, 'What a great movie.'

Yes, it is a challenge for the team sometimes, when we are constantly on show. Flare-ups happen, especially if a momentary lack of focus means something, however small, goes wrong. Maybe the relish for the candle doesn't get sent out with the bread.

Insignificant? Yes, in reality. But in the pursuit of perfection nothing is insignificant.

For sure, it changes the way the chefs work, but in a good way. You have to be neater, cleaner, try not to swear so much, but to be honest, you get so immersed in what you are doing at times, you forget that there are forty people out there who might be watching and listening.

And it's a two-way thing: it is so much more rewarding as a chef if you can see the guests eating your food.

Tom Aikens was one of the hottest restaurants in town, but downstairs in the kitchen we never saw a guest's reaction, or really felt the fruits of our work. At Per Se, the kitchen was separate, and couldn't be seen from the dining room. Yes, you will always get feedback from the floor staff, but it can't match the feeling when someone comes to the entrance of the kitchen at Story and says, 'That was one of the best meals I have eaten in my life. Thank you, everyone.' Those moments are priceless. Trust me, there is no better reward.

'You are on your feet for long hours and you have to stay focused, so it's often the camaraderie and banter and humour that gets you through. Angelo and Frank particularly like to throw themselves under the bus and bait Chef. The funniest was when Tom went over to sit down with some friends who were eating in the restaurant, and Frank got us to send him over a glass of champagne "on the house" – he turned around to see Frank in the kitchen raising his own glass to him. Of course he went ballistic.'

Seamus, sommelier

RABBIT SANDWICH

A lot of love, nostalgia and playfulness goes into the rabbit sandwich snack but I never thought it would take off the way it has, or that I would have *GQ* magazine listing it one of the hottest things to eat in London.

I used to go rabbiting with my dad and his best friend who kept ferrets – I remember a white one especially. Sometimes when they caught the rabbits they would still be alive, so we had to neck them, then the guts had to be taken out straight away, while they were still warm, and as kids we would be given them to hold: it was a bit of a rite of initiation.

Dad would bring the rabbits home and make stew for everyone: the rabbit went in the pot with loads of vegetables and some bouillon, and then we would eat it with crusty bread. It was the only thing he really cooked, but he loved it, and so did we.

The rabbit for the sandwich is a classic confit that reminds me of dad's stew, starting with lots of diced onion sweated blonde to give a base layer of flavour. It's shredded as for rillettes and shaped into fish fingers – fish fingers, sandwiches: childhood associations – then they are glazed with a tarragon emulsion, made with Minus 8 vinegar, oil and reduced chicken glaze.

In an emulsion there needs to be a protein to hold together an oil and a liquid. Usually it is an egg, as in a mayonnaise or a sabayon, but I didn't want that egginess that you can sometimes taste – instead there is enough protein in the chicken glaze, and it keeps the flavour intense.

Rabbits always eat carrots in cartoons. So we lay three slices of red, yellow and orange heritage carrots on top that have been lightly pickled with bergamot, just for a week, to flavour, not preserve them, and to lend acidity to the snack.

'Tom sees and hears everything, even when you think he isn't listening or watching; it's as if he has an extra sense. Everything about Story reflects his personality: inspirational, cheeky, playful, always driving to improve and pushing on to bigger challenges. Non-stop, right to the limit.'

Ursula,
general manager

THE WHOLE BEAST

What is better than winning? Winning from three goals down. Sometimes the greatest results in cooking happen when you refuse to give up in the face of difficulty, when you are struggling to understand an ingredient like wild stems in winter, or trying to raise the craftsmanship to a place where you didn't know you could go.

So more and more I find myself deliberately posing difficult challenges, in order to push us to our creative limits.

In a way meat presents the fewest challenges. As a chef you learn early on to look at the way an animal moves and has lived its life in order to decide the best way to cook the various parts of it.

Meat is muscle. The legs and the muscles from the front part of the animal do the most work. They are tougher, full of connective tissues. So you want to cook them long and slow – braise, roast, confit – then the collagen in the connective tissues becomes gelatinous and flavours, lubricates and tenderises the meat.

The lazy muscles, from the middle or the back of the animal – like sirloin, fillet and rump – aren't used much, so they are softer and more tender. They only need brief cooking, or the scarcity of lubricating fat will make them tough.

But when you start to explore every single part of the animal, even the bits that most people overlook, that is when I feel we are truly progressing. So nose to tail has become our mantra for the main dishes, whether it is lamb, deer, pig, quail: use every part of it, maximise the potential.

Saturday

It's always going to be tough when you put a new dish on the menu, especially in a restaurant like Story, where we work to only set menus and things need to go out of the kitchen in quick succession. It's a lamb dish and we are using the whole animal in different ways. Angelo has been talking to farmers about different breeds and we have gone with hardy Herdwick sheep, which are native to the fells of the Lake District, where they graze wild, growing slowly and producing really full-flavoured, lean flesh.

There's a lot to do. We confit the belly and shoulders and braise the head and neck for a 'head cheese': we pull out the meat, season it with salt and pepper and wild ramsons and make a ballotine, set it, cut it and bake it with brioche on top. We break out the muscles of the legs and marinate them along with the loins in sheep's yoghurt – homage to a Middle Eastern technique which allows the enzymes in the yoghurt to break down the meat a little and tenderise it. Then we roast the legs and loins and rest them; and use the bones to make a sauce.

Four lambs a week to be butchered and prepared, working two days ahead all the time. Butchery is a skill-set that I really value in the kitchen. Tom Aikens first taught me, and Angelo spent time working in a butcher's shop, which is a great way to learn – but if you put a whole animal in front of most of the young chefs who come in for a trial and said,

'Break it down into five or six cuts,' they wouldn't know where to start. That's OK, though; sometimes it's good to work with a blank canvas. What matters in a new recruit isn't necessarily what they know or where they have worked, it's about their attitude to learning and their work ethic.

When lamb first comes on the menu it signals spring, things are warming up, flowers are coming out and ramson is in abundance. Just before it goes to flower, it has little berries on it, almost like capers, that we pickle and served with the lamb, and salad leaves that we grill, because I want that slightly charred flavour.

For a chef, putting on a new dish is like going from playing left back to centre back. Everything is just a little bit different; it takes time to get used to it and you can practise and practise on the training ground, but when it comes to match day, anything can happen. So there is a different kind of urgency in the kitchen today; everyone is on edge. Me too, but I am trying not to show it.

The hot section of the kitchen is clearly behind. Angelo is looking tense, but doing his best to look after the boys.

9 a.m.

The briefing before the lunchtime service. This is when we get together as a team. Communication is everything. Today is the day that Raymond Blanc is coming in for lunch. We discuss where he will sit, and the changes on the menu. The energy is high, and I remind everyone why we work eighteen hours a day, a hundred hours a week: to give our guests the best possible experience. To be the best we possibly can.

11.45 a.m.

By noon the restaurant is full and the food is flying out to the tables. Raymond Blanc arrives looking relaxed. I am aware of every noise, every word, every movement in the kitchen. Control is the key, but you must never lose the soul and the passion.

The next two hours are draining. Service is slower than it should be, the boys are getting behind on the new dish and I know it isn't as good as it could be. I have to be the problem-solver, the leader, no point in flying off the handle. I have to stay calm, move chefs round like pieces on a chess board, step in and do the plating-up myself, and take Jon, who is in charge of the front of house aside, and say quietly, 'Be patient. Don't keep coming into the kitchen and asking for the food, because you'll only make things worse.'

The truth is our guests probably don't feel any of it. They've had a good time; they're happy. But we know, and Raymond Blanc knows. He senses it has been tough, and there is a big level of understanding there. 'It happens. I've had many difficult services in my career,' he says afterwards.

It's frustrating, but we are human. I know that everyone was trying their hardest and I can't ask for more. Scuba, the chef de partie in charge of cooking the meat, is devastated. 'I hate having a rubbish service, Chef. I'm sorry it didn't go well.'

I tell him and everyone we have to draw a line under it and move on. We just have to be better in two hours' time when we start all over again for dinner. Ultimately at the level we work at, we can't make mistakes. We have to get it right.

What makes me proud is that I don't need to say any of this. They all know. People ask me what is my greatest achievement so far, and it is this: getting this group of thirty people in the kitchen and on the floor to care so much, to know the standard, and not compromise.

Just as I am thinking this and grabbing a glass of water at the bar, I hear a smash behind me and turn around to see a chef tossing pieces of a broken plate into a box underneath it. These plates cost £80 each. I look inside the box and am devastated to see about £500 worth of broken crockery.

This time, I really am angry, so angry I punch the counter and smash my little finger. The pain makes me even more frustrated. Accidents happen, and the chefs don't know the massive pressures on my shoulders, the need to keep things tight and not be wasteful with money; I know that – but just chucking the plates into a box is not normal behaviour. I hate dishonesty, or when people cut corners or do stupid things and think I won't notice. I call my senior chefs and my restaurant manager together.

 – *Was no one going to tell me? What was the plan: wait until we had no fucking plates left, and then casually mention it?*

 – *Sorry, Chef.*

I go outside to calm down.

I don't believe there is anything wrong with losing your temper sometimes, but when I come back I apologise.

I think that is one thing that I am good at. I do react from the heart, kick off sometimes, of course I do, but I make my point and never let it fester.

At the end of a grumpy service, if it's a collective thing I pull people together for a team talk. If my anger is aimed at an individual I'll take them aside after a few minutes and give them the reasons why I behaved as I did. That's important.

If I've made a mistake or misjudged a situation, I'll say so. If something happened beyond your control,

just tell me. Then it's over. Reflect. Move on. I never want a negative atmosphere or resentment building up. But I have high standards, and those standards have brought us to where we are now.

In an hour and a half we are ready for service again and this time it all goes well. The new dish isn't on the menu. I think we pushed it on too quickly. It was my decision. I thought we were ready and you don't always get it right. We'll take a few days to refine and refine it until we get it as close to perfection as it is possible to be.

'Rome wasn't built in a day, but then again I wasn't on that particular job.'

Brian Clough

2

Market

I don't have to get dressed because I went to sleep in my clothes. When I do that it gives me an extra twelve minutes of sleep. And yes, twelve extra minutes counts! He is already on the phone, 'Are you on your way?' *3 a.m.*

   – Yes, Chef.

My brain is on autopilot, telling me to start the engine of the van. I open the window a little to help my eyes peel open, turn the heaters on full, and the radio to maximum volume. It's a short drive to pick up Tom Aikens and then another ten minutes to get to New Covent Garden market.

The market. Wow. Those two words taste of hurt to me, even now.

   – Hurry up, come on, what's wrong with you? You're tired?

Tom as always is on a mission. He's going at a million miles an hour.

   – We need to get to the French garden first! Make sure everything you choose is perfect, no bruises! Then hurry round to the mushroom man and I'll meet you there. And fucking stack the crates properly this time!

   – Yes, Chef.

My hands would be blistered from the old wooden crates, and in winter, it would be freezing. It gives me the shivers now, thinking about those icy mornings. A chef doesn't need to go to market. Trusted suppliers deliver produce to your kitchen door. But Tom believed that the market trained the mind and the body. Choose the produce, get to know the growers, the sellers, the packers. To be the best you must have knowledge.

Did an apple taste better because I picked it out? Probably not. But when I handled it later in the kitchen did I appreciate it more? Most certainly, yes.

Once, in a year and a half of going to market, perhaps eighty times, I overslept, and we didn't go. Tom was angry, and I wanted to say, 'It was only once, in all this time.' But I didn't, because once still wasn't good enough in Tom's book. I saw the disappointment in his eyes and I felt that I had let him down.

Only when you push yourself to the limit of every element of your craft will you gain a true understanding and appreciation of it. That was the lesson that Tom was teaching me.

I was seventeen years old and extremes were already an accepted part of my life.

   – Right, are you all packed and stacked, Little Tom?

   – Yes, Chef.

Into the market cafe: same order every time: two teas, marmalade on toast for Tom, a bacon sandwich for me.

Four minutes, then back to the kitchen.

Pressure

In Tom Aikens's kitchen I went from a boy to a man.
Tom is the greatest chef I have worked with, a true
inspiration and most importantly a friend. I have
nothing but respect for him.

At that stage of his career all eyes were on him; the
feeling was that this guy was going all the way to
three Michelin stars. His restaurant was rated
number eight in the world, and his food had more
soul, love and attention to detail than anything that
was going down in any other restaurant in London
at that time. I truly believe that. So we were all
under so much pressure. We probably lost a chef a
week. Some guys didn't even last a day. They would
say, 'I'm just going out to get something,' and never
come back. The intensity of Tom as an individual
was reflected in his food. He never cut you any
slack; it was unforgiving in his kitchen. Some dishes
would have ten, fifteen, twenty components, and the
level of skill and concentration required to achieve
that was relentless. If you lasted at Tom's you could
work anywhere.

It was every man for himself; we were all surviving,
so we'd be doing petty things like hiding spoons and
containers and trays from each other, so you didn't
get caught out. No one wanted Tom coming at you
because you weren't ready. When we had cleaned
down the kitchen on a Friday night ready for the weekend, I used to wait until everyone had gone home,
and then stash utensils away in the roof of my fridge.

You couldn't take a minute off. Service was so focused and fast. Relentless. Tom would only call away the checks (handwritten orders) once, then he would keep them, so you had nothing in front of you to look at. You just had to remember. Does that make sense, really? Was it a control thing, or did he want everyone to think and concentrate and focus at an elevated level. Luckily for me, I was young and I have a very good memory.

There was one dish of rabbit with carrots and parsley, that sounds simple, but it was so complex; that was the nature of his food. This dish consisted of rabbit loin, rabbit blanquette and twelve pans of garnish: pickled carrots, baby carrots cooked in carrot juice, baby roast carrots deglazed in veal jus; carrot obliques roasted with baby onions and deglazed in veal jus; carrot purée; carrot dice with carrot sauce made from carrot juice, parsley linguine, parsley gnocchi, parsley sauce, and wilted lettuce leaves to order. We worked in pairs in Tom's kitchen and I worked with a chef called Giles. Giles cooked the meat and I looked after the garnish and every time two tables in a row ordered the rabbit, we were in danger of going down. Tom was so particular, each garnish for each dish had to be cooked in an individual pan; so if you had two orders for the rabbit you had to have two pans of each garnish on the go, and you would be caning the pot-washers: 'Hurry up with the fucking pans; my life depends on it!'

And I still have nightmares, genuinely, about not being ready in time with the garnish for a dish of John Dory, cauliflower and cucumber that was on the tasting menu. Tom's food was always stunning to the eye, and each plate had to have three little 'turnovers' made from clear discs of green cucumber jelly which you set on trays in the fridge until they were like PVA glue, piped a dot of white cauliflower purée in the middle of each one, folded the jelly disc in half over the top, and again, into a quarter. If you had sixty guests you had to make 180 of them in a kitchen that was always red hot and full-on. Chefs would be banging into you and there never seemed to be enough trays.

On the nightmare night I remember counting up how many John Dorys we had left, and how many jelly discs, and saying to Giles, 'We're short on the jelly discs.'

  – *No, no, I made loads.*

  – *Are you sure?*

  – *Yeah, I'm sure.*

The last three checks came in and we needed nine John Dory, but we were three jelly discs short. Giles and I are looking at each other, thinking we might as well sign our death warrants now.

  – *You have to make some more. I'll try and slow things down and tell Chef you've gone to get something from the back.*

So I'm grabbing cucumber jelly from the fridge, melting it, then shutting myself in the walk-in freezer, cling filming the floor and starting to make the discs. Outside I can hear Tom wanting to know where I am.

  – *He's getting lemons, Chef.*

  – *Don't lie to me. What's he doing?*

I'm on my hands and knees piping the last bit of cauliflower and folding the discs, praying, 'Please don't let him come in. Please don't.'

Tom is shouting, 'I need the jelly!'

I come running in with a lemon in one hand and the discs behind my back. Did he guess? I honestly don't know, but if he did, he didn't say. I remember sitting on the bus going home, thinking, 'How the hell did we get away with that?'

We had a foie gras dish on in the summer. It was stunning, served in a massive glass bowl. Tom would sear the foie in a pan then pour chicken consommé over it, which poached it, then the consommé would become the broth. My job was to make the garnish that went into the consommé so it became a bit like a minestrone: three little pea raviolis, confit duck tongue, three spears of asparagus, split peas, split broad beans, some flaked duck and loads of herbs, so I would make them all up and have them in individual boxes ready to go.

The second the foie went into the pan if you didn't have the consommé to hand, Tom would lose it. I remember one night, he was saying, 'Consommé. consommé.' I knew if he had to say it a third time, I might as well give up, but I was late with it. He took it off me, poured what he wanted, and then poured the rest all over the section where I was working. So now it is going to take me ten minutes to clear up the mess and I have no more chicken consommé. I have to get another batch from the freezer and defrost it . . . and he is going to be swearing at me for the next ten minutes.

When stuff like that happened you would go home feeling so deflated, but then you would come in the next morning, and Tom would show you a brilliant new dish we were all going to be doing, and you would just be thinking, 'Wow. I am the luckiest guy in the world to be standing next to him, sweating with him, watching him work, learning and absorbing. He can throw me in a bath of chicken consommé if he wants! I don't care! This is fucking amazing.'

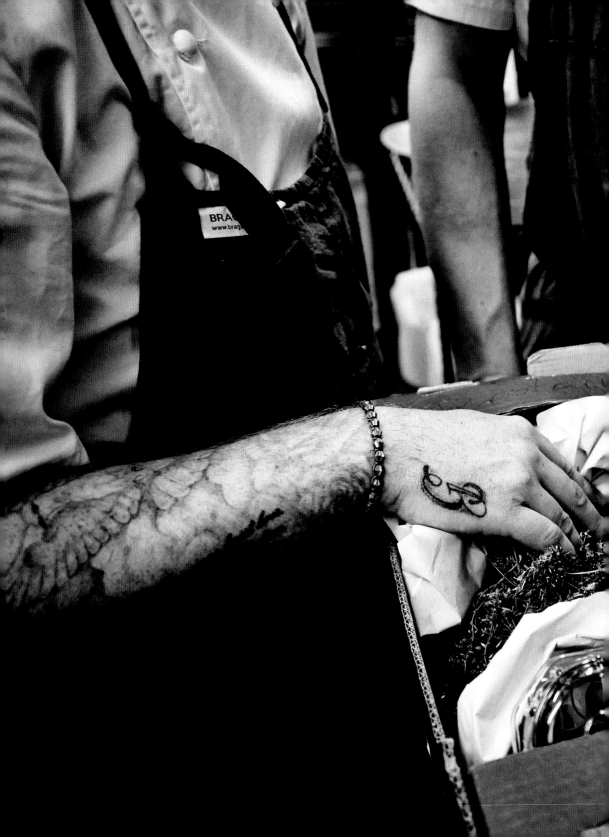

Tom taught me at such a
young age to imagine.
So my dreams were all:
what will my food be?

Tom didn't want me to open Story when I did. He worried that I was too young and it was too soon; reminded me that from the moment you open your own restaurant there is no turning back – never again will you have that pure pleasure of cooking without any other responsibility. Until the day I retire from this business, I will never have a day off. Physically, yes, but in my head, no. Because ultimately Story is my house. If it falls down everyone else can move into a new one, but I'm the one left homeless.

It must have been hard for Tom to think, 'Why isn't he listening to me all of a sudden?' But I had to be my own man, and if people truly care for you, ultimately they support you.

Winning the Michelin star, my parents coming to eat on the opening night . . . I have had a few proud moments in the last couple of years, but Tom coming into Story for dinner probably surpasses them all. He waited and waited and waited, until I was quite pissed off that he didn't come in, but he said he wanted to give me time to get it right. And I'm glad he did. Finally after we had been open for a year he showed up. What did he think? As usual he didn't say that much. But I hope he was proud.

'Probably only a handful of chefs who have worked in my kitchens over the years have had what it takes to become a great head chef or restaurant owner. Great talent doesn't come along that often: people who truly stand out from the crowd.

Tom Aikens

Tom was definitely inspired by what we were doing. He had this huge determination and a very good work ethic. First in, last out, always asking questions, looking around . . . was there something else to be done? Always ready to step in.

I could see that he was set on accomplishing something in his career, so I was willing to help him make the next steps up the ladder, to gain experience in other kitchens outside the UK, away from his comfort zone, because that is really what makes someone stand out.

I understand him, because I was exactly the same at his age, but I didn't have that father figure to guide me. As you begin to mature as a cook, and when you have a very creative head, it gets more and more difficult to take orders. It frustrates you, because you have all these ideas of your own.

Tom always said, 'When am I going to have a restaurant?' and I said: 'Hold fire, hold back for a couple of years.' If you have talent and drive, opportunity will always arrive. Someone will find you and give you the key to the door.

But he made the choice to hit the ground running and of course he's worked his arse off. His will to achieve was as strong as mine. I know what it's like to have super-high expectations, and a fear of failing, at a very young age. It's a lot of weight and stress on your shoulders. You have all the tools, apart from management, but ultimately it is mental strength that carries you over the line.

I like to take him down a peg or two – nicely. He wanted to beat my record of two stars at twenty-six, so I rib him about that occasionally.

What I say to him is to listen to people he respects, keep growing in knowledge and maturity. People give advice because they care. I am always only a phone call away.'

Sunday

Most chefs I know just sleep on their days off. We don't live within the rules of normal society; the hours we work, the limits we push ourselves against are brutal. In the winter you go to work in the dark, you go home in the dark. You can't just decide to go and see your friends for a couple of hours on a Wednesday night, or go to yoga or the gym. You work eighteen hours a day and then you stop, exhausted.

It can make you quite an angry individual, unless you find a way to channel it. I channel it into food, but am I always a happy human being? No, not always. I love going to work, I love my job, I love what I have created, the magic within the kitchen, my restaurant family, but at times it's a world of hurt and pressure.

A lot has been sacrificed to be here: friends at times, family at times, relationships at times. But it gives you the determination that you can't fail – or else what is it all for, when you ask so much of your body and your mind?

Some days my whole
body aches:
my shoulders,
my hands,
my feet,
my knees.

Monday

We are closed on Mondays, so officially I am off, but ultimately I am never off. The phone and the texts and the emails never stop.

Three sugars in my tea this morning. I know. Too much sugar. You should see the Ninja coffees the boys make for me later in the week at work, when it gets to Friday and Saturday.

My flat is full of lined notebooks that I use to make notes and lists, and drawings of new ideas. I embrace all technology but I'm old-school when it comes to writing and sketching. My latest notebook has a picture of a John Dory on the front and I'm doodling the progression of the brain of a chef from cook to restaurateur.

The first brain is full of food, the next is fifty per cent food and fifty per cent ordering and costing. The third is crammed full of figures and financials, people, management, agents . . . all the things that distract you from the place you started. Now I have to find pockets of time where I say, 'OK, for the next three hours all I am going to do is work with food. Ignore the phone; ignore the emails.' I understand why some chefs, further down the line of their careers, want to go back to their roots and take over a pub or a little local restaurant where they can just cook and cook.

In the evening I have steak and chips with some Béarnaise sauce, a little green salad on the side, and a glass of red wine at one of Jason Atherton's restaurants. I love steak and chips done well. Who doesn't? It's just what I want to eat on my day off. If I had a menu with all the food I want to eat on it, it would be steak and chips with Béarnaise sauce; beans on toast, and treacle sponge and custard, probably. And maybe a jacket potato with tuna mayo and black pepper, and a little bit of red onion. And my mum's lasagne.

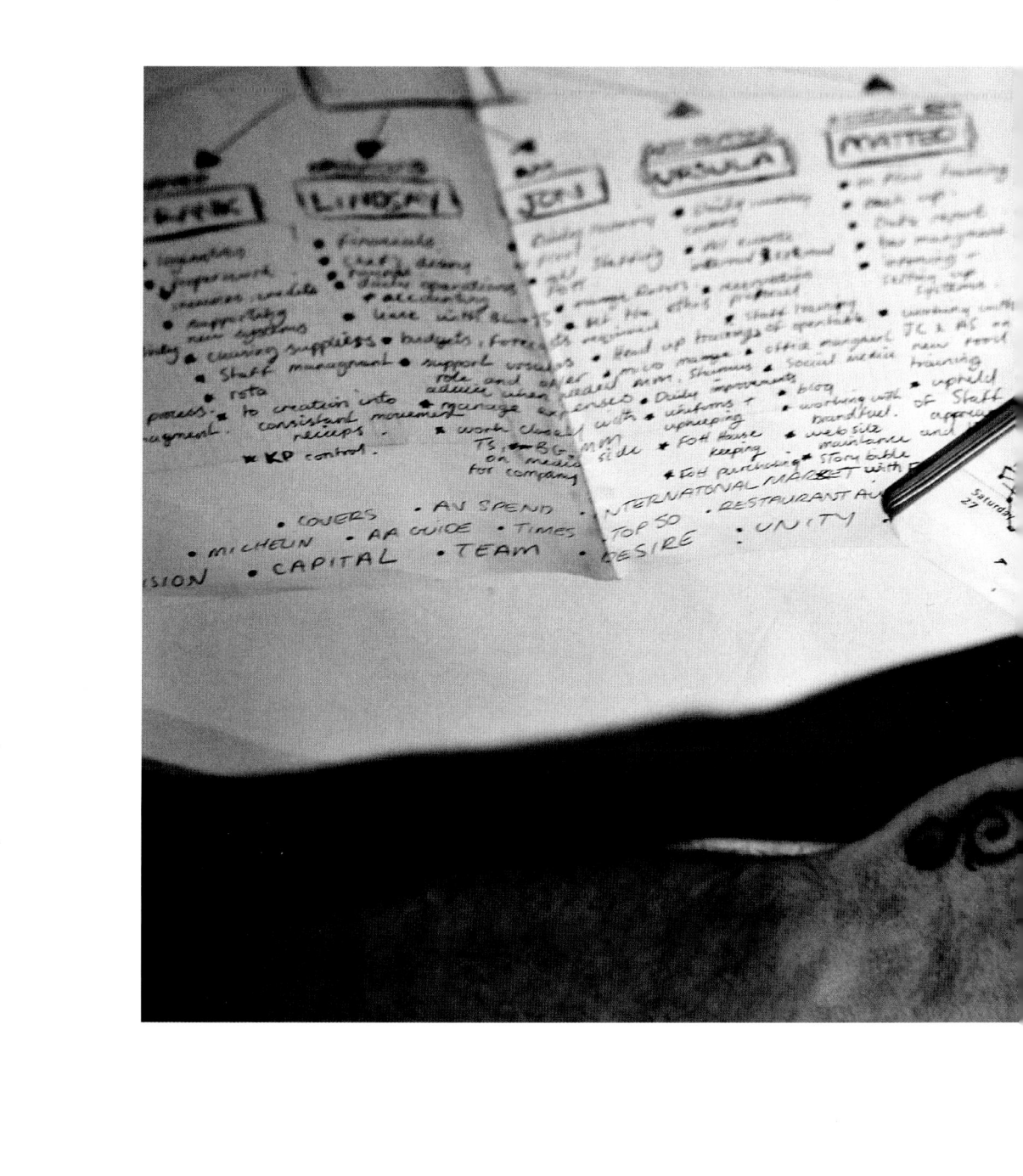

CDP

No question, your best times as a cook are the chef de partie years.

Chef in charge of a section.

It's the best and hardest job in the kitchen.

All you think about is food.

You have to remember everything; hold so much information in your head. Constantly.

Cook, cook, sleep. Repeat.

Knives, stove; the rhythm of the kitchen. You become lost in your world.

Your fridge is like your mirror, a reflection of you. Look into it and that is who you are. Those years are unbelievable.

And you have to know that once you move up to become a head chef, or ultimately have your own restaurant, you will never get them back.

The irony is that every chef wants to open a restaurant so they can cook their own kind of food, not someone else's. Continue the dream.

The reality is that there is way, way, more to it than that.

Exhaustion

I cried a lot of times in Tom's kitchen, from exhaustion probably, but every single tear was worth it, because he taught me to imagine food, to dream. And from our conversations since, I believe that he knew what he was doing all along. He knew what he wanted me to go on and achieve.

After about six months in his kitchen I remember getting on the night bus and crying all the way home. I rang my mum. I would never ring my parents in the middle of the night unless I was at rock bottom. Mum was already worried about me because I had lost so much weight. I reckon I was seven and a half stone, wet through. Nerves, stress, long hours, not eating properly . . . Sometimes I would grab some food from a late-night store on my way home, but mostly I lived on bowls of cereal.

One time, on my break after the lunchtime service – which should have been fifteen, twenty minutes – I went to the nearest cafe and ordered a coffee, sat in one of the massive comfy chairs and fell asleep. The next thing the manager was waking me up and it was six o'clock. Twenty-eight missed calls on my phone. I'd been asleep for two hours. Let's just say service was tough that night. Everything I did, I was in the wrong.

Now Mum was saying, 'I'll get in the car and come down to you.'

– No, I'm fine.

– Tom, you don't have to do this.

But I did. My dad's voice, as always in my head: 'Don't give up.' I woke up at six the next morning and didn't get out of bed. Tom was ringing my phone non-stop, leaving messages: 'Where are you, Little Tom? What's going on?'

Amazingly he showed up after service at my dingy flat.

– You've got two choices. The easy one is to go home now. The hard one is to come back tomorrow, and I promise you, I will make you the best cook you can possibly be.

Tuesday

Seven chefs with a total of twelve Michelin stars on one table. Before service begins I purposely lose my cool. It's a tactic. Premeditated. FG always jokes about my ability to turn emotion on and off. He knows now when it is for real, and when it is calculated, but the others don't. Tonight is important and I need everyone to be totally focused.

6 p.m.

I've told FG everyone needs to be upstairs and ready for the briefing at six, but some of the chefs are still in the downstairs prep kitchen and I use the fact they have missed my deadline as an excuse to turn up the heat and remind individuals, in no uncertain terms, of their responsibility within the team. Rightly or wrongly it gets the result I want. When it is show time and the big table of chefs come in, everyone is super-charged.

Wednesday

The head of the AA Guide and a writer from the *New York Times* are in for lunch today.

Jack, the apprentice, has taken his ultimatum seriously, spoken to his parents and made a decision about his future. 'I really want to be here, Chef.'

7 a.m.

I feel hugely proud of that. Being creative with food is the easy part, compared to managing a collective of people with different personalities, sensibilities, talents and skill-sets to share your vision and belief, and create a sense of team unity and spirit that is unbreakable.

Psychology probably makes up eighty per cent of my role: trying to engineer people to work to their optimum. Nobody teaches you how to do that part; though I've watched some masters.

I want them to know that my door is always open if they need to talk to me.

But you walk a fine line between being the boss, and a friend.

Let them know that you have walked in their shoes. Go out for a few beers on a night off, but leave two hours earlier.

I don't want them seeing me dancing on the tables, thinking, 'He's a dickhead.'

Sometimes you play the father figure, the confidant.

'Chef, I'm having a tough time with my girlfriend, she's not seeing enough of me.' OK. Take Saturday off, I'll cover for you. 'Chef, I'm broke.' I'll lend you some money – give it back when you can.

But it's always important to keep control. If you don't have control, you have nothing.

This business has given me the pleasure of working with chefs and front of house people with unbelievable talent and together I want us to push beyond anything we thought it was possible to achieve.

But nobody is bigger than the restaurant.

Including me.

'We're a young kitchen
with lots of passion and
we love what we do.
There's a lot of banter
and fun going on, but
young cooks can get tired
and tetchy by midweek.   Angelo,
                           head chef
If things are getting
tough sometimes Tom
will send out for pizzas
for everyone after service.'

PYP

I call it, 'play your position'.

There's a reason why I have eleven chefs in my kitchen.

My role is to identify individual strengths, then get people to play to them, to know their role within the team and stick with it. That way the whole team is better.

I am only as good as the people around me. Ask any prolific striker why he is able to score so many goals and he will say it is because he has great people behind him all over the pitch.

SALT

Every chef has a personal yardstick by which they can tell a good cook: how you poach an egg, trim an artichoke, bone a fish . . . mine is soup.

In a bowl of soup I can see if there is an understanding of individual flavours, seasoning, body, texture, acidity. Soul.

If I just blended peas and stock, yes, I would make soup, but it would be watery; no structure, no viscosity. A good soup is a very worked product.

A soup is all about building layers of flavour, so you need to season at every stage.

Seasoning is the tool chefs live or die by. Taste, season. Taste, season.

'Season to taste' in a recipe. What is that? Meaningless unless you understand what seasoning actually does.

I don't see pepper as a seasoning. It's a spice. So seasoning, to me, means salt.

Salt doesn't only develop and enhance flavour. It does so much more.

Salt draws out moisture. Sometimes you want it to; sometimes you don't, because drawing out moisture affects texture and colour.

That's why you have to apply it to every layer.

If you just cooked everything, blended it, tasted it and added salt at the end, it would be as if it was just sitting on the top. I can tell straightaway when someone has done that, instead of seasoning through the process.

Say you're making a pea soup. First step, take your onions, thinly slice them, sweat them gently in butter and add salt straight away, because you want to bring out the moisture now. Salt = more moisture in the pan = less contact between the onion and the pan = onions that stay blonde.

Onions sweated without colour are there to build structure and body in a dish. They're not there to add their own flavour, but to be a carrier for others. You don't want them to char and caramelise and colour and develop their sugars, or they will take on a whole different roasted flavour, which they would do if you cooked them hard and fast with no salt. Or long and slow, as in Lyonnaise onions, when you want all the sugars to develop more slowly, making the sliced onions taste even sweeter. Again no salt, because if the moisture comes out first, the onions will stew before they caramelise and you can taste that stewed flavour. When we make the onion dish with gin and apple, charred and Lyonnaise is exactly what we want. But not here.

Back to the soup. Add the peas, sweat them together and taste again, maybe add some mint. Then add the dairy element and stock. Let's say equal parts milk, white chicken stock and water. Taste again – remember stock will usually have its own salt.

Blend it and finish with some lemon juice for acidity. Acidity needs the structure you have built up with the help of seasoning for it to work properly. If you just squeeze in lemon juice at the end, there will be nothing rounded about the flavours, no soul, just sharpness.

Every time you think salt, think moisture.

If you don't season a steak until after you have cooked it, the salt will just sit on top of the flavour, divorced. If you salt it just before you cook it, the salt will penetrate the flesh and enhance its flavour, with no time for it to act and leach out the juices. But if you salt it and then the phone rings, and you come back to it fifteen minutes later, it's a different story. When you eat that meat it will be tougher because you will have drawn the moisture out of it.

With fish I think the opposite way. I like to season fish after cooking, just little flakes of sea salt, sitting on top. Same with a raw scallop. Because I want the separation. I want to taste all the natural, delicate flavours in the seafood, and then the salt.

OLIVE

There is nothing I like about olive oil. Or olives. You didn't expect me to say that, did you? Aren't all chefs meant to love olive oil?

But everyone has a dislike they can't get over. So you won't find olive oil in my food.

Everything changes, I know, so maybe in ten years' time, I will say my favourite thing is eating olives and I'll be researching olive oil producers. But not now.

People keep telling me how once they hated olives and then they were converted. Like my mum. She couldn't stand them, now she could eat fifty straight up.

Believe me, I try olives in every variety all the time, waiting for that game-changing moment.

I've spent years cooking with olives and olive oil in other people's kitchens. Tom Aikens had a dish with black olives, black olive oil, black olive crumb, black olive mash, and I had to keep tasting it, and all the time I was thinking, 'I fucking hate olives.'

But I am in love with rapeseed oil. When I taste olive oil all I get is bitterness, but with rapeseed oil, I get that very English just-mown-lawn smell of summer, that childhood memory of going out to play football at school just after they have cut the grass. It just makes me happy.

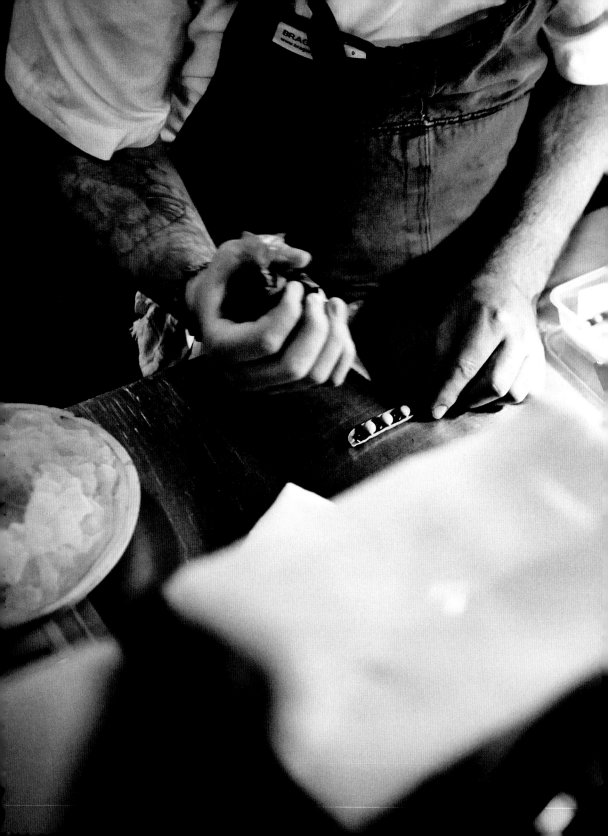

Thursday

I'm sitting talking to a journalist at one of the tables in the restaurant and I've got one eye on the boys, heads down in the kitchen. Sir Alex Ferguson said that he thought one of the biggest strengths a manager can have is sometimes to just observe and do nothing else. It's one of the hardest things to do, because you naturally want to get involved. But if you are in the middle of things in the kitchen, head down working, then you are blinkered; you can't see things as clearly. So I try to give FG and Angelo a lot of responsibility and power, take a step back and watch the way they handle things. It's another learning curve for me: how to let go, but still be in control.

11 a.m.

We've had three days now of working on the new lamb dish, and it is back on the menu again. I have had to remember that when you create a dish, just because you have a clear vision of it in your head doesn't mean everyone else is going to get it straight away. But now they are getting to grips with it, and things are calmer. I'm teasing FG who is trying to impress an attractive young lady supplier, and over the head of the journalist, I see Sam, a.k.a Scuba, frantically wafting a big plume of smoke with a tea towel and hoping I won't notice. It makes me laugh.

Scoob got his nickname because there was something about his posture that just made me think of Adam Sandler dressed up in wetsuit and flippers as the Scuba Sam character in the movie *Big Daddy*!

– Hey, Scoob, please don't set fire to the restaurant.

– Just a bit of fat, Chef!

Friday

The *New York Times* journalist enjoyed himself so much earlier in the week, he comes back a second time. The boys in the kitchen are understanding and beginning to love the new lamb dish as much as I do, *5 p.m.* and that is my reward. I feel blessed to work with them. It's as simple as that. They are the start and finish. Without them there is nothing.

America

Whenever I start to feel comfortable, I have to make myself feel uncomfortable again. After two years in Tom Aikens's kitchen I wasn't looking into the eye of the tiger any more. I was Tom's 'go-to' guy for new chefs: 'Little Tom will show you . . .', 'Ask Little Tom . . .' I could handle the rage, understood it, because it was never premeditated, it was born of pure passion, it was a measure of how much he cared. In the end I kind of loved it, courted it, needed it, it was an addiction almost, because I thought, 'I want to be like you.'

There's a big question people always ask about how far it is legitimate to push someone in the pursuit of excellence. Is there a psychological barrier you shouldn't cross? In any high pressure situation, if you can't take it, there will be fallout, people get damaged. But if you want it enough, I think there is a point of complicity between you and the person who is pushing you through every mental pain barrier. Everybody breaks at some point; the question is, 'Do you want to go again?' Because every time you do, you come back stronger.

Tom would never let you rest, he could make you feel like you weren't good enough, quick enough, responsive enough, organised enough, but he also knew when to turn things around and make you feel you were part of something special. I was in. Hooked. Bring it on. And I am one hundred per cent grateful. So in answer to the question, how far can you push someone to achieve success, I say: all the way, right to the edge and back.

My dad taught me to be tough, and later Thomas Keller and René Redzepi taught me to see the world of food and kitchens in different ways, but in terms of making me strong and focused physically and mentally, it was all about Tom Aikens. Without him I wouldn't be here at Story doing what I am doing. No question.

The fear became more about disappointing him. The day I told him I wanted to leave I was petrified.

– Why the fuck do you want to leave?

– Chef, I've been here a long time. I've worked every section. I love your food, but I want more challenges.

It was a difficult conversation. Probably the first time since I arrived that I wasn't going to say, 'Yes, Chef.' A lot of people would be bitter, but he understood that everyone has to walk their own path. And it was the first time he had ever really praised me.

– Tom, you might be one of the best cooks I have seen ever, at the age you are at. You can go and do anything you want, if you want to.

An hour later he would be bollocking me, of course he would, but Tom Aikens had just told me I was talented.

– You should go and work for Thomas Keller at Per Se.

– Why?

– Because he will take you to the next level. In order to gain that edge that will make you stand out you need to go outside your comfort zone, out of the UK.

The other side of the world. No family. No friends.

OK. Let's do it then. If Tom had told me to go and work at McDonald's I probably would have done. That's how much influence he had on my life back then.

Two days before I left for America, he invited me for dinner at his place. Afterwards he made strong English tea and got serious.

– *Remember to be fast, clean, smart. Listen!! Be the first in and the last out every day. Put your head down and do me proud. Don't let me down.*

That was an emotional moment for me. Tom had given me the tools I needed, taught me to imagine, believe, work hard and never give up, yet he had the humility to point me in a direction that would take me beyond the things he had taught me. He believed in me enough to help map out a career path for me. I felt that I stood for something, and my nerves turned into pride. I can fucking do this.

POTATO & COAL

My dad prided himself on making the best mash ever. He didn't – he'd just bash up the potatoes and butter in a pan – but we all loved it anyway. 'It's amazing, Dad.'

No other single ingredient inspires me with so much love as the potato. It is the first ingredient I really learned to understand at a serious level.

So often it is seen as a vehicle or a sideshow and not treasured the way it should be. 'Let's put some potato with this fish or that meat . . .' No. Let's make the potato the complete focus.

The romance is in having the courage to take something so humble and treat it with the love and respect it deserves so that when people taste it, it blows them away.

No fish, no meat, no bells and whistles: just potato mashed with butter and milk, and a vegetable that changes through the seasons from asparagus to peas and broad beans, radish, turnip. It has probably become the best-loved dish at Story, certainly the one that surprises people the most.

For me there is a powerful romance in bringing together potato and coal.

Potatoes, for a long time, were the working man's vegetable, fuel for families who could afford little else. For the miners working to provide a different kind of fuel from the coalfields that used to be all around Nottingham where I grew up.

Coal is a mineral underground; potatoes grow underground, surrounded by minerals. It makes sense to me.

Coal infused in oil as a flavour? What is that? I wanted that distinct taste of something that has been on the barbeque just a little too long, a little bitter, that makes you think, 'Do I like it? Do I not? I'm not quite sure.'

Mash has to start with the right potato. I found it, grown by a one-man band, Chris Hazeldone in Cambridgeshire, on chalky loam that was worked by his grandfather and uncle before him.

The man just loves potatoes. He has been involved in farming since he was about four or five-years-old, and when I first tried using his Désirée potatoes for mash, they were just the best: such a great flavour and balance of sugars and starch.

Chris is a very down to earth, modest, quite introverted guy, and if you ask him what the secret is he'll say it's nothing more than being meticulous about the fundamentals. But when I told him I wanted to put a dish on the menu that was all about the beauty of the potato he was the happiest guy in the world.

As always I think about the way an ingredient has grown up, and that hugely influences the way we treat it. The potato grows in the dark in the earth. Its skin gives it its nourishment all its lifetime, so why would you take off that skin, and throw the potato into water, an environment it has never been in before? Instead we bake each potato slowly in its skin wrapped in foil, so all the flavour, vitamins and minerals are captured inside.

There's no recipe that dictates x amount of butter and x amount of milk. It's all about understanding the potato. Put six potatoes into the oven to bake and every one will come out slightly differently, because each has its own levels of starch and sugars, which will also change the longer the potato is stored, because the more it is kept, the more it loses moisture.

Whereas the less developed the sugars and starches, the harder the potatoes are to work with, since they will take up less butter and milk when you come to mash them, so they will be less silky.

Speed, temperature and delicacy are key. Work as quickly and as little as you can, before the potato cools. The more you work it the more you activate the starch and the potato will start to become gloopy.

Push it through a potato ricer or mouli once to keep the starch molecules as intact as possible.

Then start to incorporate the fat.

First, fridge-cold, diced butter which melts into the potato before it becomes oily. A bit at a time, until it feels as if the potato would split if it was asked to carry more.

Taste and season, but only with salt. Salt brings out the flavour, pepper is too dominant.

Next, warm milk, a bit at a time, just enough to create a texture like soft putty, then pass the mash through a drum sieve, pushing, not scraping, to work the potato as little as possible.

The sieve traps all the tiny potato particles, leaving the mash smooth, shiny, silky.

I had potato and I had coal oil, but there had to be something to soften the interaction and draw them together, so we made a beurre blanc and whisked in dandelion vinegar, for that little bit of acidity that would cut through the fat of the butter in the mashed potato.

What made me think of dandelions? My mind was on potatoes and coal and fields, and I thought of walking past millions of dandelions in spring and summer when the flowers come out.

No one ever seemed to do anything with dandelions, but it gave us the touch of acidity that the dish needed to counteract the fat of the potato.

A week before we opened I told my mum I was putting on a dish of potato. She was unimpressed. 'What? And that's it?' she said. Then she ate it and changed her mind.

Polenta

I remember the exact details of everything that happened.

At Per Se the polenta had to be made and set in a block. We were going to turn it out, cut it into fingers and fry it.

I asked for the recipe and one of the sous chefs gave it to me.

I made the polenta and put it in the fridge to set, but when I went back to check it, it was still wet.

I was running to the fridge and checking . . . it was still too wet . . . running and checking . . . still too wet. It must be right; I was sure I had followed the recipe exactly.

Six o'clock and everyone was set up, ready for service. The first guests were arriving.

The polenta had to be right . . .

I took it from the fridge, turned it out and it collapsed everywhere.

In Thomas Keller's kitchen so many people worked at different levels to support each other, put up safety barriers, work in precision and harmony so nothing could go wrong. But it had.

The five senior chefs stood around me. I remember the looks on their faces. They didn't have to say anything. No one humiliated me, but I felt humiliated. They put artichokes on the menu instead, and re-printed all the menus.

The commis chefs who normally went home at six all stayed behind until eight to prep the artichokes for me. I felt bad for them. But we were a family and team unity and spirit was second to none.

No pans were thrown, there was no shouting or kicking. For me it was a huge personal failure, but what I learned was how they dealt with a problem in Thomas Keller's kitchen. There is always a solution.

Fear

I think you can learn more when you have fear.

Fear of disappointing.

Disappointing yourself and other people, people you
look up to.

Per Se

In Thomas Keller's kitchen at Per Se there was no physical fear, no shouting or bullying; but all the time I worked in the pressure cooker environment of Tom Aikens's kitchen, I had never feared anything as much as falling short of what was expected at Per Se. The fear came from letting Thomas down, letting the team down, not being good enough. This was a different kind of pressure, the pressure of having to be perfect, or as close to perfect as it is humanly possible to be.

I was only eighteen in New York, and massively lonely at first, but I could see why Tom had sent me there.

Thomas found greatness not only through his food but by making everything perfect and special for his guests, and he did that by going to huge lengths to create an environment where every system and process, from the front of house to the kitchen, was structured and organised to an unbelievable level. He would never compromise, no matter what. Thomas doesn't just set the bar. He is the bar.

When Thomas was in the kitchen, you felt you were in the presence of excellence.

The chef de cuisine at the time was Jonathan Benno, who had worked for Thomas at the French Laundry in California, and now has his own Michelin-starred restaurant in New York, called Lincoln Ristorante.

Chef Benno ran the kitchen, but Thomas was the General. Always calm, he would walk around, giving little pointers, directions, 'maybe we should look at changing this . . .' As a young cook peeking my head over the stove, I was in total awe of the ease with which he seemed to run everything. If he spoke to you everything he said was so clear, precise and thought through.

His food was a reflection of him: immaculate, clean, balanced, intelligent, based on classical cookery, but with utmost respect for every ingredient. Essentially it was three things on a plate; never over-complicated on the palate – Thomas's food always left you feeling like you could eat just another forkful, another spoonful. But the craftsmanship involved was stunning. Signature dishes like quail in a jar, foie gras torchon, or ratatouille – with all the vegetables fanned out – were mammoth tasks to make.

I think about that a lot. Craftsmanship. If there is a way I want to progress our cooking at Story, it is to introduce more craft into our work. We like to celebrate the natural side of food, but we also have it in our hands to make really beautiful things, and every now and then I think it can be quite special to present our guests with some extraordinarily complex work.

In Thomas's kitchen it was all about working for each other. That was reflected in every detail, down to the huge pride that was taken in preparing the 'family meal', the plate of food that everyone ate at 4.45 p.m. every day. That impressed me so much that we do the same at Story. Every day something nutritious and wholesome, from a stew to green curry with rice, is prepared for everyone to eat before the evening service begins.

I grew so much as a person in the environment of Per Se. You have no idea what working in a world-class kitchen can do for you in terms of life skills, of the way you carry yourself as an individual. To be surrounded every day by twenty-five to thirty of the most professional, talented, ambitious, dedicated young chefs imaginable was massively inspiring, and challenging. All of them were hungry for the same thing as me: to one day have their own place where they could cook the food they believed in.

My mantra was always: look to the chef on the left of you, look to the chef on the right of you, and aim to be better than both. Be quicker, cleaner, listen harder.

I felt hugely privileged to be a part of that ethos. And proud of myself, too, that I didn't end up like all the teachers predicted when I was at school!

There were days when I just thought, 'Here I am, at eighteen-years-old, in New York City, working in one of the best restaurants in the world, and right now Chef Benno is talking to me with the utmost integrity about how to portion a fish properly. Telling me to respect the fact that I am working with an ingredient that has grown up in the ocean, been brought to shore by a fisherman who may have battled the elements to catch it, then sold to us. And now at the end of its journey, we need to do it justice.' Wow. My real love affair with fish began right then and there.

The workload and the hours seemed like a walk in the park after Tom's kitchen, because they had an a.m. team and a p.m. team, so you only worked a twelve-hour shift and then you were supposed to finish. But I always wanted to work double shifts. I couldn't get enough of what I was learning. First in, last out; be the best, make Tom proud.

Chef Benno used to say, 'Go home!' but I'd stay on and watch and ask questions, or help out in the private dining room.

He was a huge influence on me. He taught me so much about discipline and organisation; about the relationship you need to have with yourself and the people around you. How to be professional; a young man with humility and high standards. That ambition without control can be destructive.

I think he believed in me. Maybe because he too began his career washing dishes at sixteen. He always used to say, 'Tom, when you open your own restaurant, one day you'll look over and see some old guy sitting at the bar, and it will be me. So you had better be ready.' He hasn't come to Story yet; but I know he will.

Memo to my school teachers. I asked Jonathan Benno to send me something about my time at Per Se that I could put in this book.

Anything
good,
bad,
funny. . .

This is what he sent:

'What Tom lacked in culinary experience and maturity he more than made up for with egotism and bravado. Over time, he demonstrated incredible drive, work ethic and the desire to learn. Tom was never satisfied with his work and always pushed himself to do a little better today than yesterday. I am very proud of Tom and what he has accomplished. I look forward to watching him excel for years to come.'

Chef Benno

Focus

In Thomas's kitchen the pressure was all about not making a mistake. The level of focus and attention to every little detail was awesome.

If you splashed a tiny bit of something on your jacket, you changed it. If you peeled a vegetable, you put down a piece of parchment paper first, then picked up the peelings with the paper and put them in the bin. It was probably ludicrous in terms of cost, but it kept everything meticulously pristine. The attitude wasn't, 'clean, clean, clean', it was 'never make a mess in the first place'.

The detail went right down to all the things you never thought important. You had to be clean shaven every day. Every day. If you had a bit of a beard from the night before and tried to get away with it, you would be sent downstairs to shave. You had to polish your black leather clogs every morning.

Labels had to be written always with the same pen, always in the same way on green tape, which had to be straight, and cut, never torn.

In the grand scheme of things, does it really matter if every radish is exactly the same size? Does cutting the green tape instead of tearing it ultimately have any bearing on the food that goes out to the dining room? Is it that important whether a chef has shaved every single day before coming to work? No; but everything was about training the mind to be perfect. The thinking was, if you can't keep yourself tidy and organised, and have respect for yourself, everyone and everything around you, how can you produce immaculate food?

In Thomas's kitchen I was definitely veering towards OCD. I had always had it in me to be obsessive about organisation. But the way I began stacking everything in straight lines in my fridge took it to a whole new level!

Mise en Place

'Right, there are sixty-four jobs and they all have to be done by lunch time.' That pretty much sums up mornings in a top-level kitchen. People often say to me, 'Why do you have to start at 6 a.m.?' Well, you don't just stroll in before lunch and do a bit of cooking. It's all about the mise en place – literally, 'putting in place': ingredients, the prepared components of a dish, equipment, everything where you want it ahead of time, ready to go. Organisation. Order.

It's like having a massive puzzle in front of you and you need to juggle and prioritise the pieces so that everything comes together on time. Each job demands a different level of thought, labour, skill, concentration, whether it is making pickles, picking herbs, chopping vegetables, making stocks, braising meats, marinating, portioning. Some tasks have to be spread over days. To salt and confit a veal belly takes forty-eight hours, then it has to be pressed for another six to eight hours. You can't come in on a Tuesday morning, and say, 'Right, let's get the veal belly on.'

So you build your plan and for five hours every morning you run with it, but of course nothing ever goes to plan. The first hour is the most important; it sets the tone for the day. Inevitably things happen, go wrong, throw you off course. Every day. You're working with another chef and he oversleeps, the veg van gets stuck in traffic and arrives at 9 a.m. instead of 7 a.m., something you are cooking catches and burns and you have to start over. You need to be reactive, think on your feet, improvise.

One of the things people don't necessarily understand about a kitchen is the degree of accountability that is required from everyone at every level. Every piece of the jigsaw is important and the responsibility is huge. At Story we have guests coming in who will have waited three months for a table, told their friends they are coming, are ready to spend a lot of money, to have a great time, so I can't have someone saying, 'Sorry, Chef, I forgot to order the squid.'

When I worked in Tom Aikens's kitchen I used to write my mise en place list for the next day sitting on the night bus home after service; for a start it kept me from falling asleep and missing my stop. You had to get the bigger jobs on the go first, anything that needed long cooking, and there would always be at least a dozen purées of different vegetables to be made, maybe carrot, celeriac, pepper, broccoli . . . While those were prepped and cooking you started the next job. Then one hundred scallops would come in and so cleaning those would be an hour out of your morning. It was controlled chaos; so much to be done, and how you got to the finish-line was pretty much up to you, you just had to get there, and that was a massive pressure.

Most of the flashpoints in any restaurant kitchen, verbal or physical, come from chefs being stressed, tired, emotional, under pressure to finish a job. In that state the tiniest thing such as someone taking your last container or cloth, or your plates not being where you expect them to be, can flip you over the edge.

The things we fought over at Tom's were insane. Once someone smashed a tray over my head because they needed to dry some ingredients in the cool of the oven first thing in the morning, but I had it already turned up high for something else. It's crazy what you can accept as normal behaviour. Imagine working in an office and someone comes over and smashes a keyboard on your knuckles because you used their coffee cup.

Then I went to Per Se and I was blown away by the element of control. In Thomas's kitchen it was never possible that you wouldn't be ready on time because the culture was that there would always be people to find a solution.

Two people were employed just to check in vegetables, put them away, and keep stock of them. You would say, 'All the radishes have to be this size,' and they would spend all day making sure every chef had the exact produce they needed. No running to the supermarket to buy avocados for the lunchtime menu because the order hadn't arrived, or wasting valuable time on the phone screaming at a supplier to find out where the artichokes were. Even if those guys had to drive to the other side of the county themselves, your vegetables would be there, ready, waiting for you. I was blown away by that.

If you plan, plan, plan for success, then you are probably going to achieve it. I think that was Thomas's thinking from the very beginning. Mise en place.

Pass Quotes

I print them off and tape them to the pass where we plate the food with the special bright green tape we used in Per Se: inspirational quotes that could be from sportsmen, lines from a film, Winston Churchill, Oscar Wilde . . . every day a different one. It isn't about who said them, it is about what is said. About progressing, never giving up, playing as a team, following our dreams.

Everyone stops to read the pass quote. There is something quite romantic about that. We embrace the ritual massively; it plays a big part in our lives. Sometimes someone says, 'I want this one, Chef,' and I have my favourites that get recycled.

The pass quotes are something that Thomas Keller started at Per Se and I loved the idea. The daily quote was a focus point, a way of continually inspiring himself and everyone around him. As always, the green tape had to be absolutely straight, cut with scissors, never torn. For me it put into perspective the incredible thought and detail that went into every factor of getting people to work together to produce excellence.

That green tape is a huge Thomas Keller thing. You can't even buy it in this country. We get it shipped over from America. It sticks on wet and dry surfaces, it peels off easily and you can write on it, so we use it for all our labelling. But it's not about any of that, it's about where the idea comes from and what it represents: that ethos of a team of people striving continually to be the best is one of the biggest things I took from working with Thomas.

Everyone in his kitchen wore the same butcher's blue apron, the sign of a commis, of learning, to show that everyone should be treated with equal respect and decorum, and no matter who you were, even if you came from a two Michelin-starred restaurant, you started at the bottom, because you had to learn every aspect of the kitchen. You knew the hierarchy, but there was no outward badge.

When I was at Per Se, it had been open for six years. I'm sure at the beginning it wasn't all harmony, there must have been times when Thomas felt he had failed, but you can clearly see from his ethos, mentality and personality, that constantly wanting to be better and better and better has brought him to where he is.

So now I am obsessive about green tape and pass quotes. We all wear blue aprons and I insist on the family meal. Every day when things frustrate me, I feel we are miles away from Thomas's level of excellence, but I am privileged to have seen that standard, and even though right now it feels out of reach, hopefully we will get closer and closer. And in time why can't we even equal it?

Wednesday

I just sent a text to cancel the meetings I had planned for this morning: 'My restaurant is flooded. I am in a world of hurt right now.'

10 a.m.

I can't think of anything else to say.

Yesterday water came up into the downstairs kitchen, and the guys with the pumps have only just turned up. For three days I will have to close the restaurant. That means two hundred cancelled bookings and tens of thousands in lost revenue.

Just me and Lindsay sitting in the empty restaurant, and a pumping lorry outside. The guys doing the work keep disappearing and Lindsay is taking no prisoners.

  – *Tom, that guy in the lorry is asleep. I'm going out there . . .*

I call her the operations manager, but she doesn't need a label. She makes her own role.

Sometimes gaining more control means learning to let go where you can, to trust other people to help you realise your dreams. Lindsay is the backbone of everything we do at Story. She's a friend, a shoulder to cry on, a confidante. She knows when to speak up and when to just listen. She's the ultimate team player, direct, very funny; she keeps us all grounded.

We first met the year before Story opened; when Lindsay was working front of house at a London event. She thought I was just this cocky guy who was talking about opening his own restaurant, but I was determined to do everything I could to bring her aboard.

Six months later she was my very first employee.

'Tom is like the annoying and cheeky little brother I never had. I feel quite protective of him.'

Lindsay,
operations manager

FISH

It is one of the most magical ingredients that the world has given us: the most delicate, romantic, and naturally beautiful.

Every cook has their obsession, an ingredient they fall in love with, and fish is mine.

On some strange level, I feel I have a deeply personal relationship with it. Maybe because I am a Pisces.

The irony is that they say that the world's oceans are barely five per cent discovered, so actually I probably don't know a lot about fish at all.

No ingredient challenges and tests me, surprises and frustrates me in the same way, maybe because fish is so unforgiving; it demands the utmost respect, focus and care or it kicks back at you.

For a start there is so much variety in the world of fish, from oily through white and massively meaty, all the way to the queen of the ocean, the turbot. And you have to treat each one differently.

I've cooked alongside some of the best chefs in the world, and they would probably say they had mastered cooking fish, but I don't feel I have, because I am never satisfied. But I embrace that. Frustration is a good thing. It excites me to never give up.

How do you do justice to a species that lives a life

we can't really understand? We know about cows and sheep and pigs because we rear them, we know what they eat and how they live and exercise – but even though it is possible to farm fish, what do we really know about their lives? Maybe that is part of the mystery and the romance.

Or maybe it is so challenging because it is one thing to cook a single piece of fish perfectly, no frills; but to bring it into an intelligent plate of food without it playing a passive role and becoming secondary is more difficult. If you cook a big piece of meat and serve it with horseradish and vegetables and potatoes, it stands up to it. But how do you empower something as delicate as a fish in the same way?

When I structure a dish, I am thinking, 'How can I protect the fish, keep it as natural as possible?' That is a bigger challenge than you would ever imagine.

Maybe we have nailed it, and it is just that with fish I will never feel the sense of completeness that I do when we serve the potato and coal, or the onion and gin. Perhaps I show it too much reverence ever to be satisfied with any of the fish dishes we have had on the menu.

Sea trout with gooseberry; cod with Alexander; mackerel with strawberries and salad root; mackerel with cobnut and sloes . . . our guests might say they loved those dishes, but I have a constant battle going on in my head: have I done the fish justice? Have I allowed another ingredient to get in the way of the beauty of it?

There's a classic way to cook a piece of fish, of course, by roasting it quickly in a hot pan with a little oil so that the outside caramelises, but the flesh is tender and stays moist inside, then finishing it with foaming butter and lemon juice. But only a dense, meaty fish like cod or halibut can stand up to that. And it's not my favourite way. As always I like to look at the way an ingredient is brought up. Obviously fish live in water, so my instinct is to surround it with moisture, not to subject it to the harshness of the stove. When something is so fresh and beautiful, I want to do as little to it as possible.

A delicate fish like turbot I would put in a steamer, coated in a little rapeseed oil: a barrier of love against the heat.

An oily fish, like mackerel or sea trout or salmon is more forgiving, so I would poach it in oil, gently like a confit, until it is medium rare.

Fish and chips? To take something so delicate, dip it in batter and fry it is the opposite of the ethos I have towards food. I understand that done well the fish steams inside the batter; yes, all the flavour can be there, yes, it can stay juicy and not be overcooked, but for me there is no romance in a battered fish.

Possibly the best dish I ever ate was at Noma: a fillet of pike, marinated in dill oil and wild herbs, grilled within a blanched cabbage leaf, which charred and turned crunchy and kept the fish moist and fragrant and protected inside.

I look at the whole culture of sushi and sashimi and I think maybe fish is just so special we shouldn't do anything with it at all. Take it from the ocean and eat it, that's it.

Mood

My mindset, where I am in my personal life, the weather, all these things are hugely influential in the way I cook.

If it is cold and miserable, and you need a cup of tea just to warm your hands on, I want to make food that is warm and welcoming.

If it is bright and hot, and I pass people in shorts and sunglasses when I walk to work, I want dishes that are light and happy and fun.

And it probably sounds weird, but I think I cook better when I'm pissed off at the world.

Because then I feel I have something to prove.

Ever since I started cooking, I have needed to prove things to myself. Work at a great restaurant, then another, and another. Work harder, achieve more. Eat up pressure. Show yourself you can do it.

Bravado is what I do.

STOREO

Always, when an idea graduates from notebook to kitchen, we work as a team. Someone will pitch in with an alternative ingredient or a different technique, and sometimes, if it looks like we are not winning, you just need people to say, 'Chef, it's not going to work. Give up.'

But then I'll probably say, 'I'm going to make it work.' Or the other way round.

Storeo is only on the menu because my team wouldn't give up on it.

It started with me being a fan of Oreo biscuits when I arrived in America to work at Per Se. It was winter and New York was freezing. I lived in a little room with only a bed and a wardrobe. I had a packet of Oreos by my bed, and I used to live off them and cereal with milk.

I thought it would be fun to make a version that people would recognise, but that would be savoury, not sweet.

The ingredient I wanted to use for the white filling was eel. Such an English thing, eel. So we made a smoked eel mousse. That worked.

Then we spent months and months trying to get the biscuit right. We made so many fucking biscuits.

They needed to be black, so we added squid ink to the biscuit mixture and finished it with vinegar powder. But there is so much fat and protein in squid ink, it changed the consistency of the mixture completely.

When you make a shortbread-style biscuit mix you part-bake it in a tray then stamp out your shapes and finish baking them. But the biscuits would crack and crumble if we cut back the fat too much, or refuse to set, if there was too much.

We changed and changed the ratios of ingredients; used different flours, tried baking at different temperatures.

Three weeks and hundreds of failed biscuits later, and I decided, 'We are trying too hard. Maybe we should just pack this in. Revisit it another time.'

But Fran and FG said, 'No, we can get this right.' They worked away at it, a bit each day, until ultimately, they got the balance right. True teamwork. It made me very proud.

Brother

I was in a taxi on my way to London City Airport, flying to Edinburgh to help Tom Aikens prepare for a TV cookery show. When I looked at my phone there were six missed calls from my mother.

What I heard when I called her will stay with me for the rest of my life. I could hardly understand what she was saying between the tears and screaming. My brother Oliver had broken into the house and was being violent. I heard my brother say, 'What are you ringing Tom for? He has never been here – I'll just pull the fucking phone out of the wall.'

That was the last thing I heard. The line went dead. For the next few hours I felt completely helpless, until I landed in Scotland and picked up a message from Mum, saying that she was OK and Oliver had left.

I talk about the moments of pain, exhaustion, tears and pressures of this crazy life that chefs lead, and people say, 'It must be hard,' but while I was forging a career for myself in New York, my brother's life in Nottingham was spiralling downwards into a world of drugs, violence and pain. My brother has had a gun held to his head, and one time when I went to find him we had a maniac come at us with a bottle of acid and a hammer. So let's put things into perspective. Aching limbs, lack of sleep, cuts and burns, or having the odd hot pan thrown at you in a restaurant kitchen isn't hard. Guns and hammers and acid. That's hard.

I have never really talked about this before, let alone written it down, and you might say, why am I doing it now and what has it got to do with cooking anyway? But it is only now that I can begin to understand that in some complicated way the void in my life, and the guilt and hurt I felt at not being there for my brother when he was in need, for not being able to stop what happened to him, fuelled the fire within me to channel all my energy, passion and dedication into cooking. It is the only therapy I know.

I've known plenty of chefs over the years who found themselves in a dark place due to a crisis in their lives, and it is through cooking – sometimes even discovering cooking in the first place – that they have worked through it. That can't be a coincidence.

Also, in some way I felt that if I wasn't there for Oliver because I was following my career, then I couldn't allow myself to fail, could I?

And if I could make a success of things, then maybe the chain reaction would have a positive effect on my brother and my family.

Oliver as he was before, and is again now, is an amazing, caring, lovely person. He has been clean for five years, works hard and keeps away from town, in case he sees anyone from the bad days. I'm so proud he is my brother.

We're like my dad, Ollie and I, we don't find it easy to talk about things too deeply, but the process of putting everything down on paper has forced us to talk about what happened, for the first time.

We lost four years of our relationship, though, and I still haven't found peace about what happened. How can two kids who grew up so close diverge so dramatically?

The world that my brother descended into was dark,

messed up, frightening. And I couldn't understand it. I have never taken a narcotic in my life, never even tried a cigarette.

I've seen one too many kids come to work in kitchens who have clearly done way too many festivals and drugs, and they can't remember anything. I'm serious. If you haven't got a memory in a kitchen you might as well give up.

And I've seen out of control, excessive things in kitchens thanks to drugs. One guy stabbed himself in the hand to get out of service, because he couldn't handle the pressure. The same guy stabbed someone else in the arse because they stole his spoon. It wasn't just drugs, one guy used to cane the drink massively: the cooking wine, the dessert wine, anything he could get his hands on in the kitchen. I remember one time he went into the walk-in fridge to get some milk, and fell asleep.

Guys would say they needed to take cocaine to keep them going, but I always thought that was bollocks. I understand how it happens, because of the pressures, the hours, the stresses, but it is also pretty clear to me that if you choose to get involved with drugs you will get nowhere in restaurants.

The frightening thing is that Oliver wasn't taking hard drugs. Someone offered him some weed one day and that was it. He got more and more addicted, until he ended up smoking it from first thing in the morning until last thing at night. It totally messed with his head, made him short-tempered, aggressive, and plunged him into a dangerous lifestyle.

On the day my mum called for help, he was desperate, on the edge. He owed some money to people who had threatened him at gunpoint. Where we grew up you know that if someone has a gun it isn't just a scare tactic.

At first I didn't even know what was happening to Oliver. My parents kept me in the dark to try to protect me, to let me focus on my career, with no distractions. So when I came home on a short break from working in America, it was a shock that he was no longer living at home and he wouldn't answer his phone.

The day before I was due to fly back to New York I walked to the local shop to buy a loaf of bread for Mum. I remember it was raining, and inside the shop my brother was standing at the counter with two other lads. We just looked at each other, like strangers. He was barely recognisable to me, ill-looking and underweight. I didn't know what to say. Then he just pushed past me without a word and left. It was probably my saddest moment.

To this day I don't know if I did right or wrong to shut out what was happening, but in my defence it wasn't until I had finished my time in New York that the true reality of my brother's life hit home.

My parents didn't want me to get involved, but I thought I was mentally tough, physically strong and so I had this ridiculous, 'I'm home now, I can help my brother' attitude. As if I could sprinkle magic dust and everything would get better overnight. I had been away for so long, I didn't understand that things had gone way past that.

I blamed myself. I had broken my dad's rule that my brother and I should always be there for each other. When he was in trouble I was away pursuing my own dreams. I had abandoned the one person in my life that I had been taught to stand by and protect. The person I thought I would never fail. Now we weren't even talking. At one point I didn't even know where he was living. There would be phone calls in the early hours, my sister calling me in hysterics, telling me Oliver was in trouble. 'You have to go and find him.' One time he was kicked and beaten so badly that his ribs were broken, he had internal bleeding and he could barely open his eyes.

My parents were in pieces. They tried everything; paid for private treatment. I threatened people I knew who sold him drugs, tried to get him to move away; pulled him away from the guy with the hammer and the acid. I didn't know what else to do.

At our lowest point Oliver and I came to blows outside our parents' house. Why were we even fighting? All I wanted to do was protect my little brother, but the truth was I didn't know who he was any more. He was a different person. The drugs had done that.

In the end, like always in these situations, I realised that the only person who could help him was himself. I know now that what brought him back to us was the love he had for his girlfriend, who is an amazing person, and stuck by him through it all.

Like I said, the men in our family don't often talk about our deepest emotions. But when Oliver came to eat on the opening night of Story with my parents, that was a massive moment for me.

Striving for perfection is about the relationship you have with yourself, your family and loved ones. Being able to look them in the eye and know you did everything you could.

3

France

Tom Aikens was classically trained and studied in the kitchens of Frenchmen Pierre Koffmann, Joël Robuchon and Gérard Boyer. So when I returned from America, he thought that I should go to France to learn a different set of skills.

He arranged a six-month stage for me at La Maison Troisgros, the famous three Michelin-starred restaurant in Roanne in the Loire region of France. I think I was the first English cook they had employed in decades, and although I liked the style of cooking, everyone was very supportive, and I wanted to learn, I wasn't happy there.

Roanne felt small, remote and quiet after New York, the language was a massive barrier for me, and in France you could only work thirty-five hours a week by law, with limited overtime. So from working long hours I had too much free time on my hands and nothing to do with it. I felt I wasn't moving fast enough.

To be honest Per Se was always going to be a hard act to follow. I had loved everything about the way Thomas Keller ran his restaurant. It still inspires me every day at Story.

Maybe I was just lonely.

I probably wasn't mature enough to express it at the time, but looking back I think I just needed some head space.

Back in Nottingham my family were going through a tough time. It all added up to me wanting to go home.

I remember walking back to my flat one afternoon through Roanne and everything seemed to be closed, and I just thought, 'I'm going to ring Tom and tell him I'm not happy.'

I should have stuck it out: head down, absorb everything. But my heart was saying, this isn't for me. Staying would have been the easier option. It was much harder to make that phone call.

Tom and I butted heads. He was disappointed, and it was his reputation on the line. I know he felt let down; sad even.

He told me to stay, give it more time, but I had made a choice and I stood by it.

But ultimately I saw it as a failure. At Troisgros everyone was rightly confused. What had they done, to make me want to leave after only six weeks? Nothing. It was all down to me.

Up until then I had been totally guided by Tom and hugely appreciative, but I had thought more about impressing him and doing him proud, than what I wanted for myself. Now I felt that I had to make my own decision, rightly or wrongly. There are many routes to your destiny, and just because Tom's had been achieved via France, that didn't mean it was right for me.

When I came home it was difficult at first, but we talked about it like grown-ups, and started planning where I should go next.

Denmark.

Tattoo

How do you express yourself when you grow up in a tough environment where showing your feelings isn't always easy?

You find ways to make a statement. I do it best through my food but tattoos are a big part of it too. I'm a very impulsive person and each one represents my feelings at a particular time in my life, traced on the body: part of the journey, always changing, and I don't regret any of them, because the feelings they represent are what ultimately will define me.

The attitude to tattoos has changed; they are so much more acceptable now, considered beautiful even, so it's no coincidence that a lot of chefs have elaborate words and designs on their arms, because of the expressive type of people we are. But it wasn't always so, and tattoos can't be hidden from those who don't think they are beautiful. I can cover my arms if I have to wear a suit for an important meeting, but not my hands. I've seen people's instinctive reactions. But sometimes I like the fact that I am saying, 'This is who I am.'

Truly, if I think about why I had them done it is because they are a silent expression of things that I sometimes couldn't, or didn't want to say. If I pass a stranger on a street, or sit next to someone on a train, they see the tattoos but only I know what they mean to me.

Love. It's an easy, obvious word, but the reason it is inked on my hand is pretty deep. I fell in love with food from the beginning, but I often wondered if I would find anything, or anyone to match that feeling. Then I met someone who had the same kind of power over me, someone equally significant. I cooked differently when I was in love. My judgement, my values changed, I was happier, more balanced. She was a rock and a support and that was reflected in my food, maybe because I stopped trying so hard. I was more relaxed. If someone on Table 5 complained, it didn't hurt so much.

Above the word love there are roses and among them two birds and one has taken the other's heart. She still has mine, even though it is over. But now maybe the significance of the word love has come full circle. Maybe it represents the fact that through everything my relationship with food has never let me down. It has brought its own happiness and sadness, highs and lows; but it is the one constant in my life. And it always will be.

I got my very first tattoo when I was fifteen or sixteen. It's on my back and it says, 'Tears reflect strength.' Then it was all about rebellion. My way of putting two fingers up to the world; going off and getting a tattoo without my parents knowing.

The next ones, the initials on my hands, show the opposite emotion: they are my parents' initials, one set on each hand, which I had done spontaneously, stupidly maybe, after everything my family went through with my brother, when I was feeling guilty about not being there to help. Those tattoos were the expression of the personal battles and challenges I was dealing with at that time.

The words on my arm, on the opposite page, are from Vince Lombardi, an American football player from Brooklyn who became one of the most successful coaches ever.

'I firmly believe that any man's finest hours – his greatest fulfillment of all that he holds dear – is that moment when he has worked his heart out in good cause and lies exhausted on the field of battle – victorious.'

Vince Lombardi

Lombardi led the Green Bay Packers in Wisconsin to five national league championships and two Super Bowl victories in the sixties. I had those words done as a reminder not just to live my life but to attack it, according to the ethos that my dad taught me: if you work hard and be honest in your work, however tough it is, you can achieve.

The artwork above it was all done freehand during my time at Noma, by a Danish woman whose natural backgrounds, shading and light touch I admired. Twelve hours of pain. But I think the result is quite beautiful and light. Even my mum likes it, though it isn't completed. There is a space where there should be a big feather.

There are thirteen roses, not for the number thirteen, but because my mum was born on the first of the month, my dad on the third. There are two doves, because they say a dove never flies alone. They symbolise the idea that there is someone out there for everyone and one day you will meet them. I still believe that.

Above everything there is a Jesus Christ figure and then the sky, which I guess is me asking, is there something out there?

Maybe one day I will finish it.

Tuesday

A week ago the kitchen team decided to pull a 7 a.m. meeting.

Agenda: to discuss ideas to help us progress, improve or change in order to become more slick, manage time or housekeeping better.

6.45 am

That made me proud.

I want them to push me as much as I push them; and they do. Even harder sometimes.

This morning Jack is in at 6.45 a.m. prompt, waiting for everyone to gather for another meeting.

Angelo and FG are looking blank, but unwittingly Jack has just driven us forward again with his expectation of a weekly meeting, same time, same place.

So now there is a 7 a.m. kitchen meeting every Tuesday morning at Restaurant Story.

'My first day in the kitchen as an apprentice, I was told to weigh out flour, vinegar, mix them together, add lemon juice, keep tasting. Everyone was laughing. Then they told me that was the mixture for polishing the copper pans.'

Jack, chef

– Scoob, what happened to your shoes, man?
His clogs are in shreds.

   – Haven't had time to buy a new pair, Chef.   *9 a.m.*

   – Scoob, do you want me to buy you a pair of shoes?

   – Please, Chef.

When you're on your feet for eighteen hours a day a shoe becomes quite relevant.

Everyone in our kitchen wears black leather Boston Birkenstock clogs with cork soles that mould themselves to the shape of your foot.

I probably get through four pairs a year. That's fifty pairs of clogs since I started cooking.

René

People always ask me about my time at Noma. What was it like working for René Redzepi, the man whose restaurant is considered the best in the world? Simple. It was like getting on a bus that was never going to stop. For anyone. If there was an earthquake, or the biggest hurricane or snowstorm in the world, René wouldn't stop.

Everyone says René is a genius, one of the greatest cooks to walk this planet. And he is. Ultimate respect goes out to him. But what is a genius? Is it someone who has an innate brilliance with food, or is it a guy who says, 'Fuck you, I am going to do what you say I can't do'? People forget he had been doing what he was doing for six or seven years, with a handful of people coming in for lunch or dinner, before he started making headlines, but he never gave up on what he believed he could achieve.

I think about that long and hard sometimes, because what I took away from Noma was less about cooking than courage. Of course I had huge respect for René's food. Of course I took huge inspiration from the way he looked at everything so differently, pushed you to think outside the box. There is no one else out there like him.

But it was his ambition, his tenacious, bullish attitude and his personal will to never surrender that impressed me massively. René was obsessed with conquering the world with Nordic food, wood sorrel over caviar, working with nothing that couldn't be found or foraged or combed from the seashore, exploring and experimenting with alternatives to the accepted cooking cultures of other countries. You wouldn't find a lemon in René's kitchen because citrus fruit don't grow in Denmark. We had to find other ways of creating acidity. His totally stubborn attitude was, 'I'm not stopping until people listen.' He found power through lack of resources. He narrowed his channel of focus so much that he made life fucking hard for himself. However, once he broke through the door, he was so innovative in the way he looked at and thought about food. It was all about identity, not fame. He didn't care about rules, he was saying, 'This is Noma, and this is the way we do things.' Some chefs set out to win three Michelin stars, be flawless, get all the accolades. With René it was purely about 'the Noma way.' If you have that belief in something and the genius to pursue it, ultimately the rest will follow.

In the restaurant world everyone wants to mark you – critics or bloggers giving you ratings out of five, out of ten, out of a hundred – but at Noma they marked themselves and that is all that mattered. I honestly believe they found themselves at Number One in the world, because they marked themselves every single day, and weren't afraid to fail in the process. That was what was even more special. As a guest in the restaurant you would never know, of course not, but behind the scenes in the test kitchens René was on a journey that celebrated failure.

So many cooks are scared to fail, but if you can embrace not getting something right, and using it as a positive, you will only ever find success. If René failed his attitude was, 'Fine, it means we're fucking trying; so let's keep failing.'

That was such an inspiration to me. Maybe the word failure should be deleted from the English language and replaced with learning. You win or you learn.

If I look at the 'failures' in my life, and I guess you could say Noma was one of them to a certain extent, they have shaped my life as much as anything else.

Working with René was never about ticking boxes, or doing things the way they had always been done, or the way people would understand or expect. If he got knocked over, he would just come back twice as hard. He taught me that if you have the tenacity and the drive and the will to achieve, nothing can stop you. It is that I thank René for, above everything.

Noma had two kitchens, as we have at Story, but they were the opposite way round: the restaurant was downstairs, and the kitchen off it was where the magic happened, where the last pieces of the jigsaw that made up each dish came together under René's watchful eye. René took the whole snack idea to another level. The snacks were awesome, and I loved that instant engagement with the guest, the excitement, the pace of this quick succession of massive flavours packed into small, amazing looking mouthfuls. So cool. I was working on the cold side and after the snacks we would often be responsible for the first five or six dishes: bang, bang, bang. It was fast and furious.

Upstairs was a relentless production line, incredibly labour intensive because René's dishes were so complex, but in that clever way that made the end result appear simple. There might be eight people around a bench just picking over wild plants from the beach, or five people doing the fiddly work of roasting tiny beech nuts, cracking them out of their shells then rubbing off the inner skins, one by one.

René's kitchen at that time seemed like a revolving door of chefs who had flown in from all corners of the world just to do a stage – a short stint – with the man who had the best restaurant in the world. There was a solid core of 'René's people' like Torsten and Lars and Victor, who had been with him for years and believed totally in everything he was doing, but they relied heavily on this constantly changing fan club of people from all different cultures. Each week there were new names to remember. It was exciting but it added to the challenge.

Maybe I imagined it or was over-sensitive, but I felt that René's attitude to me was, 'I don't care about the grandness of your CV, here we do things the Noma way,' which was quite right, but on my first day in service, I felt he singled me out: 'What the fuck are you doing?' 'Hurry up . . .' I was just trying to follow the service and learn what I was going to be responsible for.

I remember Victor the sous chef giving me a box of beach herbs and plants for a shrimp dish with sea urchin snow that I hadn't even seen, and when René took one look at them he exploded in front of me: 'Is that all you have?' To his credit Victor took the blame, and when I came in the next day and saw the box of herbs as it should have been, I thought, 'No wonder he kicked off.' We were missing about ten different varieties. But how would I know? How could it be my fault?

On the one hand the edginess took me back to Tom's kitchen and I was thinking, 'I fucking love this; I will show you I can work at this level, keep my section tight, be the best.' On the other, I thought, 'I'm not a boy any more. Why did I come here to be treated like this?'

The best moments were when René would talk to me about flavours and I felt involved in the journey he was on. I remember one Saturday after service at about two in the morning he came into the kitchen with a dozen different eggs, saying, 'Chef, cook these for me.' So I fried the eggs and we sat there tasting each one, with him saying, 'This one is creamy . . . this one is even creamier . . . What about the texture of this yolk? What about the fat levels?' When you are sitting next to probably the most creative chef of your generation in the early hours of the morning talking about the relative creaminess of egg yolks, you feel you are in a special place.

On other Saturdays after service we had Project Nights, when a chef from each section would make a dish, whatever idea they wanted, and we would sit around and discuss it constructively, what worked, what didn't. It was a way of building up confidence, encouraging people to express themselves in a kitchen which, with such a creative genius at the helm, might otherwise feel intimidating. It was an intelligent thing to do and I loved those nights.

At that time René was experimenting a lot with the 'fifth taste', umami, which was first identified by a Japanese scientist and what we now recognise in Western food along with sweet, sour, bitter and salty. He had another big project on the go, the 'fermented kitchen' and he used to ask me about Marmite, which gets its umami from a secret recipe using brewer's yeast. He was working with everything from gooseberries and apples to cabbage and yellow peas, which he was fermenting miso-style, and calling it 'pea-so' – genius; very clever.

He was under a lot of pressure, I understand that now, more than ever. Being the best restaurant in the world was draining. Almost every day some three Michelin-starred chef or other VIP was in for lunch, and René would create separate menus for different tables. Sam, one of the sous chefs, would brief us the night before on all the things we needed, to make sure we had everything: fjord shrimps, beach plants, blossoms, wild mushrooms, nuts . . . Check in with Roland the forager, or Tage, the forester who brought us leaves and sap and berries. You'd go home with a ball of stuff in your head, ready to explode.

We had one massive Saturday coming up, with some legends of cooking coming for lunch and René was understandably tense. He had a habit of playing with his bunch of keys when he was anxious, and that mood would spread around the kitchen, so we were all on edge and we knew we had to be super switched-on, not miss a beat. If he felt we weren't absolutely on it, he could lose it over some small thing just before service and tell us all how fucking useless we were: even his most senior chefs. The flip side of his genius and his obsession was that it could make him irrational. Or was it all psychology, his way of sharpening us up so we didn't make a mistake?

On that Saturday I got up even earlier than usual, about 5.30 a.m. I used to cycle to work and my route through Copenhagan took me past a statue with steps around it. I was exhausted after a long week, and my head was full of what I needed to do that morning. I wasn't concentrating on where I was going and I clipped the steps with the front wheel and went flying off the bike. My trainers were slashed and the pain in my toe was horrendous. I got into the kitchen, went to get changed, and when I pulled off my sock my toe was a mess underneath. It was starting to swell and throb, the skin was ripped off and part of the nail was missing.

Why today of all days? There was another English guy in the kitchen and he put a big plaster on it and taped it up. I smashed painkillers down through the day and tried not to hobble and catch René's eye. At the end of the night my toe was black and blue, but I got through without anyone else knowing.

I think I understood what drove René's genius, but I never really understood René the man. To me he was a big riddle. He reminded me of Tom Aikens in that he loved to make last-minute changes to dishes to keep the pressure ramped up in the kitchen, but whereas I could read Tom, I never really knew René.

I didn't buy any of the fluffy-cloud stuff that bloggers and critics used to write about this guy

who just wanted to make the world a better place through his food. The René I saw was relentless in his determination that Noma would be the best. Very Type A, so utmost respect. The problem was that I am pretty Type A myself. I have always been outspoken; if I have something to say I say it. With me it is never going to be all sunshine and rainbows. If there is a wall in front of me, I won't always walk around it, I'll smash my way through it. The way I behaved at times, the things I said, didn't do me any favours. I pissed off quite a few people, René included.

But I was learning about myself. Since I left school I had given everything to studying my craft, submerging myself in my work, neglecting family, friends, girlfriends, helping other chefs to achieve their dreams. Now I felt it was my time. So, my head and my heart were no longer in the right place to be a part of the Noma team.

Ultimately I wasn't looking for René's approval in the way I had always looked for approval in Tom's kitchen and at Per Se. I wasn't there to sign up to the René fan-club, what I wanted was to learn from him, because I had my own dreams. To this day I don't know whether he understood that, or just thought I was a jumped-up English prick.

Close to the end of my time there we were in the middle of a brutal service. I remember I was cooking langoustines, and in his frustration he lashed out. My reaction was to laugh. The wrong thing to do.

 – *How dare you fucking laugh at me?*

He told me to get out of the kitchen. So I got on my bike and went home.

I came in the next day, six in the morning as usual, and on the surface it might have seemed like things returned to normal, but it was never the same.

Noma shaped my destiny, but not in the way I, or anyone else had expected. I'm not proud of the way it ended. The worst was that René had brought in a head chef called Matt Orlando, with whom I had worked at Per Se, and had huge respect for, so I felt I had let *him* down more than anyone.

But you can't dwell on things; you have to move on. The fact is I worked with one of the most extraordinary chefs of our time in the best restaurant in the world. And what I saw in René was something I recognised in myself. It didn't work out at Noma in the way I had imagined or wished. But I could take that as a failure, or I could learn from it.

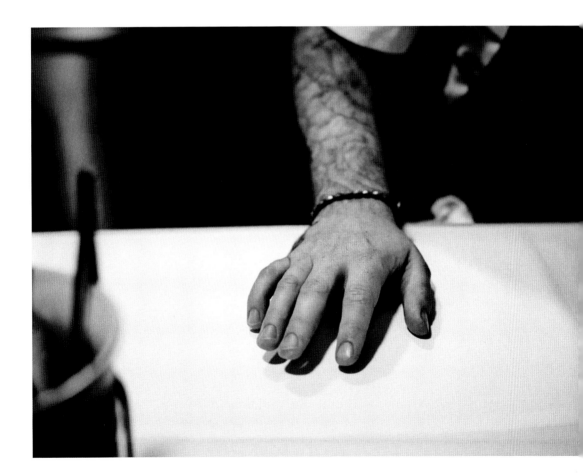

My Time

Tom Aikens first taught me to imagine, but I was imagining within *his* world. René had forged an entirely different world, created his own inimitable identity, and he opened my eyes to think, 'Why can't I have *my* world, my identity? And why can't I have it now?'

I remember sitting on the plane home after my time was up at Noma. My head was all over the place fluttering from regret to excitement, but I knew it was time to try and go it alone. I came home and told my family and friends, 'I am going to open my own restaurant.'

   – How?

   – I'm just going to make it happen.

It really was that simple. There was no single defining moment, when I thought, 'I'm ready.' You are never ready. It was just about proving to myself that I could build something and see it through. I had given myself the best possible chance by working with some of the best chefs in the world, in the best kitchens, with the best produce, and I knew I could hold my own. But ultimately I was running on youth and naivety. I just had the balls to go for it.

SCALLOP, CUCUMBER & DILL ASH

I believe some ingredients have been put on this earth never to be changed or touched, or they lose their beauty. To me a scallop is the greatest example. With an ingredient like a potato or an onion you have to tease out the best in it, and some people would argue that a scallop, too, is at its most brilliant if you roast it in butter in a hot pan in the classic way, so that the outside caramelises. But I disagree.

Everything about this dish is hugely and unashamedly influenced by my time at Noma, and René's philosophy of fresh, raw, clean flavours and the utmost respect for everything on the plate.

The raw scallops are sliced and just before serving put into a little elderflower vinegar. Last year we didn't make enough, so around October we moved on to meadowsweet, which I think of as an autumnal version of elderflower. Still quite medicinal and floral, but with a slightly different flavour.

We take the cucumber skins and chargrill them until they are completely black, dry them and spin them to make a powder that still tastes of cucumber, then we mix it with dill oil into a paste, and roll balls of fresh cucumber in it.

So you have sweetness in the scallop, acidity from the vinegar, texture and freshness from the cucumber with a little charry edge – and we add some nasturtium flowers for a touch of bitterness.

Texturally all that is very light, but what adds body and draws everything together is the horseradish cream and dill oil – two fats together, but oil is lighter than cream, so when we spoon it onto the plate they split out and marble. Then, when the two different fats with their own viscosities play off each other in the mouth, the textural sensation is quite special. I love that. It feels very elegant.

And I love horseradish as a flavour. It adds spice and heat, but in a less aggressive way than chilli. It must be that it is deep in my food memory from eating it as a child with roast beef: Colman's horseradish sauce on the table, you can't beat it.

You find an ingredient you love and want to work with it as much as possible, but not in the obvious way.

What is strange is that it doesn't abide by the rule of most root vegetables. It grows in the same way as beetroot, so I would expect to be able to cook it in the same way, but I have tried baking or roasting it numerous times, encasing it in salt, hay . . . and it is always horrible, really chewy, fibrous. There is nothing good about cooked horseradish.

But if you just peel it, grate it, juice it, and use it on its own, or infuse it in something like vinegar or buttermilk, freeze it and then make snow out of it, use it in a foam, a custard, a cream, an oil or an emulsion . . . the flavour is immense, amazing.

Tuesday

I don't think change necessarily equals progression.
Not when it is for change's sake. But if a week has
gone by and I don't feel we have moved forward in
however small a way that makes us better, slicker, *10 a.m.*
stronger, then that feels like failure.

By the end of the week, I never want a waiter to carry
more than two plates of food to a table at a time. It
shouldn't happen, but sometimes when we are under
pressure it does, and that really fucking annoys me.
It looks clumsy; it isn't a polished delivery of a dish;
and it spoils the easy interaction with the guests.

We are working on a dish with grains. Maybe barley
or spelt. I have this feeling that grains shouldn't be
cooked completely, but should have more texture. I
want them to be just beyond raw so they almost pop
in your mouth.

They need be the star of the show, but I'm going
to pair them with beef and the sloes that my dad
picked last year and we have pickled in vinegar. The
way I make food connections, it makes sense to
me. Beef herds graze on grass and then are typically
finished on grain. And the sloes that my dad picks
grow around the fields where the cows graze. That's
the romance and the narrative; now the reality of
making it work as a chef begins.

I want the texture of the beef to be the opposite
of the grains, so we are planning to cook it slowly,

slowly over three days – a piece of well-hung beef with a good marbling of fat which will melt during cooking and make the beef so soft and rich that it will virtually fall apart in your mouth.

Then we'll finish it on the Green Egg, because I still want the fire: that charred flavour on the outside that you get from cooking over coals.

Browning the meat is about the visuals too. You can never overlook the power of what you see on the plate to affect your enjoyment.

We are not in total
harmony yet.

Sometimes under
pressure you might
compromise to get to the
finishing line.

That frustrates me.

We should never
waver from what we
set out to do.

Star

Sitting on the park bench just behind the restaurant. I couldn't sleep all night. It felt like I was six years old again on the night before Christmas, half excited and half scared that Santa might not come.

26 September, 2013

I'd been tossing and turning, checking my phone for messages, tossing and turning, scanning the internet to see if the Michelin awards had been leaked. Nothing.

At 5.30 a.m. I gave up and got up, showered and by 6.30 a.m. I was sitting on the bench, trying to keep my emotions together, waiting for the list to be published at 7 a.m.

For weeks there hadn't been a day that went by without a friend, guest or journalist saying, 'Do you think you are going to get a star?' In the kitchen, everyone was wondering, 'Will we get it . . . ?' I was just trying not to think about it, telling myself we don't need to be judged by awards to know what we have achieved.

Virtually the whole of my cooking life I have been surrounded by the Michelin standard.

Tom Aikens: two Michelin stars by the age of twenty-six.

Thomas Keller: six Michelin stars.

René Redzepi: two Michelin stars.

I grew up a product of the Michelin environment, believing that the stars define you, separate you from the others. So however much I know the most important thing is to give our guests a great experience, if I have a restaurant that doesn't have at least one Michelin star, in my book I have failed.

So much stress for a little macaroon and a line or two on a page in a guide book. No big plaque or trophy.

Does the experience of cooking Michelin-standard food in other people's restaurants make it any easier in your own? Probably. Or does it make the whole experience harder? Definitely. All the more so because however much chefs reckon they know what the inspectors are looking for, do we really? It's all still pretty mysterious.

Maybe that's why the whole concept of the red book is so addictive. It's your best friend and worst enemy.

Suddenly a call comes through from Borra. 'You got it.'

  – *Are you kidding?*

  – *I would never kid about something like that!*

I still didn't believe it. I had to see it for myself. I scrolled through the list on my phone. All the names were a blur. I scanned through frantically, and then I saw it: Story. One Michelin Star.

I did a lot of crying sitting on that bench. Passers-by must have thought, 'Who is the crazy man?' I rang my mum and she said, 'I told you you would do it.' And then we were both crying.

Tom Aikens was the first to call. 'Congratulations. How do you feel?'

How did I feel? One hundred per cent relief. A massive weight lifted from my shoulders. Relief that I didn't have to go into my restaurant and pick up thirty-five people from the floor. Because that is what I would have had to do. Every single person had worked as hard for that star as me. A little part of me wanted to say, 'Fuck you, I told you so,' to a few people. But beyond that, nothing. I was numb. It was surreal; one of those emotional moments when I couldn't find the right words to say.

The rest of the day was insane. We cracked open some champagne in the kitchen, then it was back to work because we were full for lunch and dinner, but the energy in the kitchen and the dining room was unbelievable. All the time my phone was ringing, the Twitter feed was incessant: press, friends, family, all wanting to know, 'How do you feel?'

I've thought about it a lot since: that question. I should have felt elated, overjoyed, but I didn't. I think I understand it now. It was because one star in my book isn't success. All it means is that I am one third of the way there. All my life I have said, 'I want to get three stars,' and I have put a lot of pressure on myself by saying that. But all my life, too, I have had it drilled into me to never get complacent, never rest on your laurels. When people say, 'Look at where you came from, and look how much you have achieved,' that just irritates me. Ultimately one star puts you on the stage, that's all. Now it is up to us to really perform, to turn one star into two. And every September will be the same: the rumour-mill in overdrive, the predictions and bets, the lying awake wondering, wishing. Probably getting up and going to sit on that exact same bench to wait for the news.

Sometimes I wonder if Michelin truly understand the power they have over people's lives because once you get that star the level of expectation completely changes, from guests, peers, media, staff. Everyone.

And the beauty and the agony of it is you just never know when, or if, you might get a second star . . . or even that dreamed-of third. Or imagine waking up to find that a star has been taken away. It happens.

Time

Never enough.

The clock in the kitchen is the enemy; a relentless reminder of what has yet to be achieved; what isn't happening quickly enough.

But I don't even need the clock to know what time of day it is. The rhythm of the kitchen tells me, the rhythm of people all working towards the same goal.

I know it is 6 a.m. because my sous chefs are ironing their jackets. I know it is 7 a.m. because the deliveries are arriving. 8 a.m. and the bread goes into the oven.

Balancing time is crucial. Never lose a second, but be organised enough not to waste it. Pick pockets of it when you need to. Stay patient.

> 11.45 a.m. Staff briefing.
> Noon. Curtain up.
> 4.45 p.m. Family meal.
> 5.30 p.m. Second batch of bread.
> 5.45 p.m. Evening briefing.
> 6 p.m. Curtain up again.

Midnight. Another eighteen hours over and another day almost finished. A bowl of cereal and sleep. Or not.

'I love what we are trying
to achieve; I've made
a total commitment to
the dream. Where Tom
and I click is that we
are pretty similar, very
ambitious, on a mission.   Angelo,
                             head chef
We want everything and
we want it now.'

DILL & ALMOND

I fell in love with dill in Denmark. Such a Scandinavian flavour. I'd never been mad about it before but the more I tasted it and worked with it, the more I appreciated it.

I am going to serve it with almonds and it's going to be a dessert.

FG is looking at me: 'Really?'

This is the way my food brain works: if you see a young almond on a tree, it has a green fur all around it. The fur reminded me of dill. The spark of the idea was that simple. But then I began to taste it in my head. I thought about the characteristics of dill – vibrant, strong – and a fresh almond not long past its youthful, almost jelly-like texture: sweet and full of sunshine.

I put an almond and a piece of dill in my mouth and thought, 'Wow!' It was one of those ten-per-cent-that-you-can't-teach moments that brings a big smile to your face.

From there the crafting of the dish was all about contrasts of textures and temperatures.

Almond ice cream, almond butter, almond brittle, almond snow. Dill snow, dill salt, and the linking cloak: dill oil, mixed with almond oil and milk, so that it splits out and marbles green and white.

Trinity

Who are you cooking for? It's a valid question. Yourself or your guests?

I think a lot about that.

And I think that if you cook for yourself, ultimately you will fail.

What is your goal? To design a plate of food that is stunning, complex, genius, thought-provoking, that will catch the eye of other chefs, critics, guide books; or just cook something that people want to eat. It's about the balance.

Why do I cook? To make people happy ultimately. There is no better feeling.

I could have put together all my training with Tom, Thomas and René and just made beautiful food. I could go into the kitchen right now and say, 'Let's make a stunning classical terrine. Let's have an à la carte menu and work on inspired, technically perfect dishes.' But that is never going to happen. I'm not that person. I want our food to taste great and also be thought-provoking, but does that mean I would want to eat it every day? Actually, no.

Adam Byatt is one of those rare chefs who cooks the things he loves to eat; who enjoys his own food, but also understands his guests.

After I came home from France, I felt hugely jaded. What I needed was the experience of a neighbourhood restaurant, owned by a hugely talented chef whose love of cooking shone through every day.

Over a span of two years I worked with Adam twice – before I went to Noma – and again when I came home, and took charge of the kitchen for a while.

I wanted to learn about the managerial side of the restaurant business, the ordering, the financials, and Adam helped me massively.

So much of what I do on a daily basis I learned at Trinity.

Eating the Chef

Tom, Thomas, René, Adam . . . in my book each is a genius, but each running their own very different race.

In each of their kitchens there have been dishes that have blown me away; not just because they were stunning plates of food, but because they so represented their makers it was like eating the chef.

Tom's pig's head, trotters and belly, with celeriac, turnips and carrot. Based on a Pierre Koffmann dish, with all the depth of flavour that classic cooking brings, but as if it was put in a time machine and brought bang up to today, with all the added zing and zang and complexity of four or five extra components popping in your mouth.

Thomas Keller's oysters and pearls: clean, precise but generous and indulgent, immaculately and cleverly put together with huge craftsmanship.

René's dish of raw chestnuts, toasted walnut and rye, mustard cress, birch wine and butter sauce, finished with fish eggs. The accepted idea of ingredients turned upside down, very Nordic, very local, hugely intelligent, a stunning balance of freshness, fat, texture.

Adam's pig's trotters, braised, chopped, and served almost like a ragout with fried quail's eggs and sauce gribiche. Moreish, big in flavour, well-balanced and honest.

If there is a single dish that represents me – so far – it
would be the potato and coal.

'Tom in one word: complex. He is a multi-faceted being. For a short period he ran the kitchen at Trinity while Adam and his head chef, Graham, were away, which was very inspiring and quite entertaining. There was a bespoke menu, but being the egotist he is he would refer to it as a T-Spoke, with everything made to order, last minute. There was a very efficient, regimented German chef who hated it, but I loved it, and I think most people in the kitchen did. It was great fun. That was probably when I decided I could work for him.'

FG,
sous chef

Hands

A chef's hands are everything.

Good hands set you apart.

I risked mine in a stupid moment at Trinity.

I was more fiery in those days.

I was in charge of the kitchen, and a plate of food went to the wrong table. Maybe it was the waiter's fault; maybe it was mine.

I had probably worked sixty or seventy hours that week and I was exhausted. Maybe I called the wrong table.

Either way I was angry and frustrated. I hate mistakes. I had a big chef's knife in my hand, which I smashed into the chopping board in front of me in anger. But I caught my little finger under the heel of the knife. The weird thing is that it hurt no more than a pin-prick.

It bled a little, but I thought nothing of it.

I'd cut my fingers enough times before; had a lot of stitches in my hands over the years.

I lost the top of a finger one time and it had to be grafted back on. It's still sensitive now, especially when it's cold.

I dressed the cut, wrapped my finger in cling film and carried on working.

By the end of service the finger was swollen and I couldn't bend it properly. But I still carried on working.

Five days of chopping through pain and telling myself not to be weak, I gave in and said to Adam, 'I have to go to hospital, my finger won't move.'

I'll never forget the doctor at the walk-in centre at St George's Hospital in Tooting saying, 'You need someone to bring a bag of clothes for you. The surgeon is coming to see you now.' Even then I was pretty composed, until he said to me, 'You are in danger of losing the use of your finger; you have severed all the tendons.'

They were talking to me about how the tendons wither and die; asking why hadn't I come in earlier? They couldn't believe I had carried on working. The surgeon was explaining that the surgery was serious. I just lay there waiting for them to put me to sleep, thinking, 'What an idiot.' One moment of anger.

But the body is an amazing thing. The tendons had shrunk back to the base of my finger, but with twenty-eight stitches they were able to reattach them to the bone.

My finger was encased in a splint, and I had to move back home with my parents for twelve weeks, because I couldn't afford to stay in London.

I wasn't allowed to use my hand. The doctors said that if I snapped the tendons again I would definitely lose the use of the finger.

I couldn't brush my teeth, tie my shoelaces; the throbbing pan was like the worst toothache. In those three months I thought I would go insane.

It was the longest time I hadn't cooked in eleven years.

The physio told me, 'People don't realise that something so tiny can affect you for the rest of your life.' And it has. Every time, I chop, I feel it. A constant reminder.

After eight weeks, the stitches were out. I reckoned I could go back to work. Adam said, 'Just try chopping something.'

I went into my mum's kitchen, got out an onion and picked up a knife. The pain!

Four weeks later, when I returned to Trinity, what hurt most was my pride.

Now my knife skills were slower.

Maybe no one else knew.

But I did.

It was a stark life lesson in the importance of self-control.

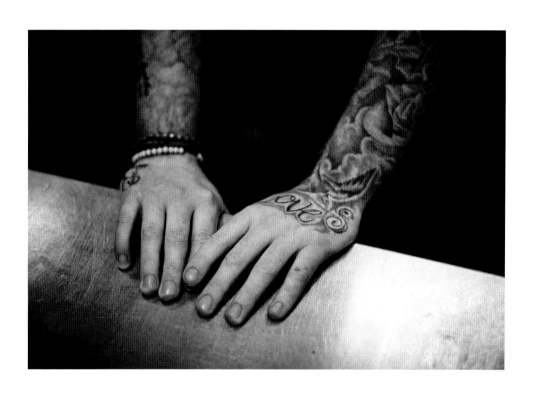

Hurt

Adam Byatt and I had so much in common in our backgrounds and beliefs. We could actually go out and have a beer and not talk about cooking. He was a brilliant friend; I knew his wife and kids, he knew my family, so I thought it made sense for us to go into business together.

I remember standing in a bar in Singapore after I had helped him put on a big dinner there, and him saying, 'I believe you can have one of the best restaurants in the world.' And me saying, 'Let's fucking do it.'

So how did we get from there to here, where we can't even talk to each other any more?

I still go over and over it in my head, and the only way I can make sense of it is that almost from the start we saw Story differently. It wasn't about who was right or who was wrong. We just had different goals. I felt Adam was looking through a magnifying glass, and I was looking out of a telescope.

I believe fear of failure affected Adam more than me. I think the age difference came into play. He had the maturity and the experience, I had the bravado of a twenty-six-year-old. Yes, there were times when I maybe should have listened more. And yes, Story is a niche restaurant. Yes, we were taking risks; probably more than I realised. But I believed. The more successful we became, the further apart we grew. Which was fucking crazy.

We were flying; we had a Michelin star after only five months of opening. All I wanted was for Adam to be as happy and proud of what we were building as me.

But he was the one person who didn't call me on the day we got the Michelin star.

That will haunt me for the rest of my life.

Things came to a crescendo on a Sunday in the middle of winter. I called him and said we need to talk. We sat in a bar in Bermondsey, and a lot of hurtful things were said.

Ultimately it was my name and reputation, and I felt that I had to be able to look myself in the mirror and say, 'I make the decisions'. Right or wrong, good or bad, succeed or fail.

I felt the right thing for the restaurant was to buy Adam out and he obliged. Money changes everything. And we don't have a friendship any more. That hurts still.

I went into a very dark place; didn't take phone calls, ignored the messages from Borra.

I never felt more lonely. Who did I have to talk to now, to bounce ideas off on a day-to-day basis?

My therapy as usual was the only one I have ever known. Cook it better. For three weeks I buried myself in food. I made a real nuisance of myself in the kitchen. I wanted to run the cold side, do the pastry; behave like a chef de partie again.

Relationships die, bad things happen, but ultimately you still have to get up every day, walk into your restaurant and carry on.

'We live, we die. And the wheels on the bus go round and round . . .'

Jack Nicholson in
The Bucket List

ACID

Sweetness, acidity, balance . . . three words you hear over and over in any kitchen. Acidity in food is key but there are different ways to find it.

Tom Aikens's cooking was very much about sweet and sour on top of classical foundations, and he found that sourness through citrus – he loved lemon juice! There were times when I went home feeling I must look and smell like a lemon!

But at Noma, because lemons weren't a Nordic ingredient we had to find our acidity from vinegars, or herbs like sorrel.

A light bulb went on for me in René's kitchen. Using vinegar and pickles can sometimes work better than citrus.

I wanted to build on that influence and inspiration, but keep it relevant to our British narrative at Story.

elderflower vinegar	sloe vinegar
pickled damsons	pickled cherries
meadowsweet vinegar	plum vinegar
bilberry vinegar	cherry vinegar
yarrow vinegar	pickled elderberries
pine vinegar	rowanberry vinegar
	rhubarb vinegar

. . . all have a place in our kitchen.

The very essence of wild plants is that nature dictates when you can have them. We love that idea of progressing dishes throughout the year using only what is free and in season. But also when a beautiful ingredient like elderflower is all over the hedgerows in spring and summer, you think, 'How can I have that all year round?'

There is something magical about using elderflower vinegar in December. Once people preserved foods this way because they needed too. Now, we are going back to the old methods for pure pleasure.

When the elderflowers are in season in early summer we bring bin bags full of them into the kitchen every day, kilos and kilos, ready for vinegar-making. The same with rose petals. You only need a dash of a vinegar made with rose petal or elderflower to split and marble a sauce or mayonnaise, or in the case of elderflower, to lightly pickle raw scallops.

In autumn we bring in medlars. They call the medlar the forgotten fruit, but I love it because it's so British. We allow them to ferment naturally, then scoop out the flesh, spread it out between sheets of parchment paper and roll it up to make a fruit leather which tastes like a cross between fig and date. We use it in our black pudding snack: wedges of home-made black pudding with a layer of the medlar leather over the top, brushed with brown butter and scattered with Maldon sea salt.

Thursday

In seconds 'the book' opens at Restaurant Story. It's a massive day. Our restaurant is fully booked, and we're about to release the tables for the next few months. The last time we did it we had over two thousand calls in the first seven minutes.

Insane.

Amazing but insane.

For a whole day the entire office does nothing but answer calls and collect data: contact numbers, names, dietary requirements, occasions: birthdays, anniversaries, proposals.

First impressions are vital. We will be judged on how slick we are, how professional.

A lot could go wrong in the time between that phone call and the guest's arrival at the restaurant so every piece of data is crucial.

All the World's a Critic

I think chefs now live in the most unforgiving era of food.

Social media has changed everything.

It's a measure of how fashionable a topic food has become that someone would even devote so much time to talking, tweeting, blogging and reviewing a restaurant and gossiping about a chef.

Yes, a bad review hurts. Every time. One hundred per cent. Even if I know the writer is talking bollocks. Human nature being what it is, if there are fifty customer reviews on a website and forty-four are written by people who have had a brilliant time and can't wait to come back again, I'll only remember the painful ones.

I say I don't read reviews and blogs any more; but that's not true. It used to be only professional restaurant critics who had you chasing a good line of opinion on a page in a guidebook or newspaper, but now everyone is a food expert and analyst. Some nights it is like being in a room full of paparazzi with phones sending pictures of every plate of food to Instagram. Even before guests are out of the door they have tweeted their opinions or posted their thoughts onto sites all over the Internet.

Every day I get tweets from people saying they are coming to the restaurant. 'Hope it doesn't disappoint.' 'Hope it is as good as everyone says.' Expectations are so high, it's as if you can't just come in, relax and enjoy yourself. The experience has to be mind-blowing or it's rubbish.

It can be vicious out there. The week we opened, a few courses into dinner service the man and two women on Table 5 started tweeting furiously, saying, 'This is shit.' And I am standing ten feet away in the kitchen, picking up their tweets. Then they left suddenly without eating dessert, refused to pay, and as they walked out of the door, started tweeting again, saying, 'You hide inside your glass box; don't even come out and see us . . .' To this day I don't understand why they left or what they didn't like.

I saved the post that hurt the most, with the line that broke my heart: 'a fine example of a young kid looking for fame first and foremost, and cooking good-tasting food second.'

Everyone is entitled to an opinion, of course. But trust me, no chef starts out cooking because they want to be famous. If you could see what most of us sacrifice along the way, if you flipped into our world and saw the pressure and the huge decisions that we have to take every day that ripple out and affect so many other people, you would know that a restaurant isn't a vanity project.

4

Friday

Angelo has just made one of the best things I have ever eaten, a new snack of raw langoustine with horseradish, and a vinaigrette made from its brains. It was simply stunning.

3.30 p.m.

Cooking knows no boundaries; only expectations.

I am surrounded by talent and ambition, and letting that grow, setting the pace and the direction, is key.

We are planning better, putting in new structures and systems to help us constantly progress and improve. I'm learning to be more patient; calmer. In the early days if I wanted to change something, or put a new dish on the menu, I wanted it now. And if I couldn't get things done immediately, I became frustrated. Even though I knew it was unrealistic, I needed certain trusted people around me to say, 'No, you can't have that now.'

So now I will listen and go away and think about it and maybe come back and say, 'You're right.'

Or, 'I'm doing it anyway.'

The Void

I've been thinking a lot about what makes a dish a 'stayer'. The way I see it you can lay down two different markers on the same menu. On the one hand you can focus on something sublimely simple and beautiful like roasting a chicken with thoughtfulness and finesse. A perfectly roasted chicken is one of the best things in the world. Fact. Or you can aim at producing something that is stunning in its complexity and craftsmanship, that takes food to a place you didn't imagine was possible. Both skills deserve the utmost respect. But in between is a huge void, and if I ever feel that we can't hit either mark on the nail and we fall into that void then I am unhappy, and however much we might love a dish at first, it won't stay. I'll want to scrap it and start over.

If you look at the majority of the combinations that will probably never come off the menu – bread and dripping, potato and coal, onion and gin, scallop and cucumber, almond and dill – they veer towards the simple end of the scale, but now I feel we are really finding our groove at the opposite end with our nose-to-tail main courses, using the challenge of working with every part of the animal to hone the craftsmanship.

Friday

Chef, can we get two stars?' says Jack.

   – You tell me?

5.20 p.m.

   – I think we can. The family is too strong not to.

I have to turn away to answer my phone, so he can't see the smile on my face. That sense of belonging that he feels means I have achieved something great. He is right. We are so strong, and we can achieve anything we want, if we work together.

My greatest satisfaction comes from the team driving me, and not the other way round. Ultimately they see it as their restaurant.

Monday

Every chef knows that feeling when you first wake up at 6 a.m.: your body feels shattered. You just want to turn over and go back to sleep.

If I don't get up immediately and into the shower I am done for.

When I worked at Tom Aikens, myself and some of the boys had a pact that as soon as we woke up we'd phone each other. You had to keep ringing until you got a 'Yeah, I'm up'.

   – Jack, how many alarm clocks have you got?

   – Seven, Chef.

   – Is there one like a rocket?

   – One has wheels, it drives off around the room beeping so you have to get up to find it. And I've got a helicopter that flies away and only turns off the alarm when you get it back on its base.

FG says, 'I had one back in the day that kept asking you questions and you had to get three of them right to turn it off. I'd be so tired, I'd just be pressing every single button, trying to shut it up.'

This morning, everyone makes it into Story on time, not for work, but for a day out at the seaside.

We are heading off on a bus trip to Whitstable for a day's plant-hunting with Miles Irving and his colleague Ross, of Forager, who supply us with wild stems, leaves and flowers. All of us, the entire team: kitchen staff, waiting staff . . .

Making a dish is only half of the experience we want to give our guests. We then have to explain it to them. It's important to me that everyone who delivers food to the tables understands what we are trying to achieve. Knowledge is empowering.

You can't run a Mercedes garage, and have your staff know less about the engines than your customers. Same thing at Story. Whoever brings your food to your table has to know not only how it was prepared, but everything about each ingredient: where it comes from, the name of every wild stem, how much longer it will be in season. They are all professionals. No one wants to deliver food to a table and be caught out by a question they can't answer.

On another level it's also quite simply about getting out in the sunshine, and having fun, growing as a team. Everyone works extremely hard, so the responsibility is on me to give back to them as much as possible.

First stop, once FG has finally worked out the directions, is a great old-school café on the seafront for massive bacon/egg/sausage sandwiches outside, with the wind whipping around us and the rows of painted beach huts stretching off in the distance.

Miles is like some romantic, long-haired prophet striding out in his long black coat with his dog, explaining that back in the day, people would have naturally known all about wild food, because human beings were just another species, dependent on the things that lived around us. Whereas now we have a weird disconnect with nature that people label progress.

The advent of farming, for Miles, was a step backwards, not forward. Now he reckons sixty per cent of the calories we eat globally comes from just four plants: wheat, soya, maize and rice, whereas a hunter-gatherer would have eaten up to two hundred different plants in the course of a year, depending on where in the world he lived. In this country alone Miles says he has identified around five hundred edible wild plants that contain a great deal of nutritional value, unlike the big four which are dominated by carbohydrate, mostly starch.

What would happen if tomorrow all the wheat in the world failed because of a universal disease? We'd be in real trouble, because we have lost the biodiversity of different varieties, and the knowledge and ability to live off the land as our ancestors would have done.

Miles has come to play an important role in what we do at Story. He is looking to kitchens like ours to help turn the clock back a little and think outside the box, to challenge and inform our guests, and start people thinking about all the wild food that is out there, largely forgotten about.

For the next couple of hours, in the space of a mile or so, it's as if we walk through two seasons: one minute we are in hot sunshine, the next it turns cold, windy, wintry, with splatters of rain.

Miles and Ross are totally in tune with their surroundings, reading signs like rings in the grass to guide them to the plants they are searching for. Ross, like everyone who works for Forager, trained for three to four years before he was even allowed to man the phones, because there is a serious aspect to foraging. Accidentally eat deadly hemlock instead of wild chervil, and it would mean a sudden end to your foraging career.

I know what I am looking for: young tender spruce, which you can eat raw and sea beet, which is just producing flower spikes that look like tiny, long romanescos – you can fry them in butter, and they go really crispy.

We find angelica, which I discovered in Iceland, where they put the raw, quite medicinal seeds into vodka; salsify buds; pepperwort – really peppery, like watercress – and dittander, which I absolutely love, because it tastes of horseradish. But I still haven't found the best way to use it, except to include it raw in our dish of squid and stems. Frustratingly, like horseradish and most of the mustard family, if you cook dittander, the flavour disappears.

Ibrahim, our Nigerian kitchen porter, not accustomed to fiery flavours, takes a mouthful of the dittander that we are all passing around, breaking off pieces to nibble. He looks as if his head is about to explode!

It's not just the pleasure of being shown so many potential treasures that most of us would otherwise walk straight past, but the sea, the changing mood of the weather and the crazy clouds, that are firing up my imagination about what I could do with certain flavours and textures back in the kitchen at Story.

The important thing, as always, is balance and perspective. Don't get totally carried away by the romance of it all. Just because something is wild and interesting doesn't necessarily mean you want to eat it on a plate in a London restaurant.

Not all of the leaves are pleasant, but others are amazing. Like sea cabbage, sea kale and awesome rapini: sweet, like broccoli, and slightly smoky on the finish. And the sea arrowgrass we find on the shore that tastes like coriander and I first came across at Noma, because it also grew on the beaches around Copenhagan.

The first time I ever went foraging was at Noma, but even then I used to be out in the forests thinking about how much more wild produce I could find back home. Look what René had achieved in Denmark – what couldn't we find from the wild in a country five times as big? I wanted to grab food in Britain by the scruff of the neck: the amazing dairy produce, beef and lamb, wonderful fruits, brilliant shellfish – and all the wild food that nature has to offer.

At Noma when the ramsons came into season we would have to go out into the forest at the crack of dawn every day to pick them. At the end of the previous night's service sometimes we would toss a coin to decide who would go, because it would be freezing cold in the woods.

René had a famous, interactive cook-your-own-egg dish, which was a huge talking point. The guest was given a basket of spinach, wild ramsons and other plants and herbs from the forest, a plate with damp hay on it, a duck egg, some hay oil and thyme butter. And a timer.

Then a hot skillet would be brought to the table and placed on the damp hay. The guest had to put in some of the hay oil, crack in the egg and then start the timer, which was set for two minutes. When they were up, they had to add the thyme butter and the spinach and leaves. You watched from the kitchen, and as soon as the eggs went into the pan, you had to set your own timer for three and a half minutes, then bring out the wild ramson sauce you had made and pour it all over the eggs and spinach. Finally the guest would finish off the dish by sprinkling on the rest of the wild plants and herbs.

As we round a corner on the last leg of our ramble, we spot a profusion of ramsons by a fence. Their tiny tight little buds taste like a cross between garlic and spring onion. They are crying out to be picked while they are in abundance, some to be eaten fresh and the rest pickled in vinegar. Magical.

'We feel like a family.
And the food is
very, very OK,
especially sandwich
rabbit.'

Ibrahim,
kitchen porter

ALEXANDER

The first time I tasted Alexander was in a field in Canterbury with Miles.

He pulled it out of the ground and said, 'Try this.'

I had never even seen it before. It looked like green rhubarb. It had the most amazing perfumey floral aroma, and when I tasted it: wow!

A little tart, a little acidic, a little like lovage.

You don't forget moments like that.

I knew I had to use it, but how?

Raw, roasted, pickled, sweet or savoury?

I brought some back to the kitchen and tried cooking it, but heat took all the love out of it, killed the flavour, turned it a little fibrous.

I tried infusing it into a sugar and water syrup. Again it wasn't good.

At last I realised that the way to eat it was exactly as I had done in that field, minus the muddy hands.

As a cook, you are always raring to use your talent, apply your craft, and manipulate an ingredient in some way, but some things are just not meant to be changed.

I looked around for an ingredient to pair it with, that would add a little protein but still allow the Alexander to be the star.

And here I broke my own rule of never allowing anything to outshine fish, and chose to put it with cod, which I felt had the right substance and body. The Alexander has such a strong, predominant floral nature, it wouldn't work with an oily fish.

We left the Alexander raw, chopped very finely, and added some English caviar for a little bit of indulgence.

Even with the addition of the caviar, this dish was all about the Alexander.

Soul

For me an amazing kitchen is one in which there is freedom of expression, underpinned with discipline, finesse, knowledge and understanding.

Musicians learn to play the same notes.

Classical dancers learn the same moves.

Artists learn the same colour palette.

Chefs learn the same techniques.

But what makes a great musician, a great dancer, a great artist, or a great chef is that extra something that comes from the heart, that extra ten per cent that you can't teach.

No one can quite put their finger on it.

But it gives you goose bumps.

Soul.

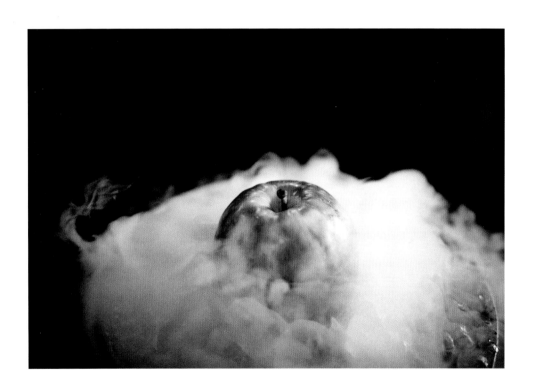

RAW BEEF & APPLE

A is for apple.

An apple a day keeps the doctor away.

Snow White and the tempting red apple: 'One bite, make a wish, and all your dreams will come true,' said the wicked Queen . . .

Apple phone. Apple computer . . . Steve Jobs, now there was someone who cared about the detail: 'Focus and simplicity. Simple can be harder than complex.'

There always seems to have been an apple in my life. In everyone's life.

I wanted to celebrate it, but keep it as intact and fresh and natural as possible. If you apply heat – bake it, stew it or roast it – you change the flavour and texture.

Now here's the way I connect apple and beef – it might sound fucking weird, but it is the way I imagine food.

I think of a crisp English apple as a ball of sweetness and acidity that explodes when you bite into it. It reminds me of the spray when a wave hits a rock. So my thought progression isn't: apple, orchard, green fields, cows; but: apple and ocean, and then, surf and turf. Though either route brings me to apple and beef. We tasted so many varieties of fairy-tale red apples, looking for the right texture, crunch, balance. Some were too floury-textured and floral. Some too tart. Finally we chose Pink Lady: not too sweet, not too tart, texturally just right.

I wanted the beef to be raw too. When people think about meat it is usually hot, even a classic steak tartare is served at room temperature. But I wanted it to be cold. Dry-ice cold.

Raw beef has less flavour than when it is roasted and caramelised, so we dice it and combine it with apple – diced and compressed using a vacpac machine, to take the air out of it and intensify the flavour – rye breadcrumbs, rapeseed oil and salt, and spoon it into the hollowed out apple.

There's something about eating out of a vessel, whether it is an apple, a cocktail glass, a cup, that demands layers. It's a nostalgic thing. From my food memory bank I am recalling an ice cream sundae on holiday; or Mum's trifle, with my dad saying, 'It needs more sherry.'

So we have a layer of shaved black truffle and a disc of apple jelly over the top of the beef, to crack through. It's a theatrical dish.

I like to watch the guests' faces as the shiny, red, tempting apple goes out to the tables in a cauldron of dry ice.

Wednesday

I've been away for four days on Mykonos. My first
holiday in years in a tiny window of time before we
start planning some major building work at Story.
Lindsay: 'You need a holiday, Tom.'   *10 a.m.*

  – No, I'm fine, don't worry.

  – Tom, I'm telling you. Not asking.

She just goes ahead and books it.

They call Mykonos the windy island, windmills
everywhere.

For the first two days I fall asleep every hour; it takes
time to even begin to unwind.

I could spend all day in the ocean. You feel so free.
When I was a kid we used to go out on boat trips on
family holidays, and I just loved that, diving into the
sea from the deck.

Sand in your toes; that feeling in the evening when
you have a shower and your skin feels slightly tight
and sunkissed. You put a cool shirt on and some
aftershave and step outside. The sun is going down
and you get a cold beer. Heaven.

I even love the simplicity and beauty of taking a fish straight from the boats, brushing it with oil, and putting it whole on the barbie. Greek salad, beautiful tomatoes, tzatziki. What better illustration of the power of the moment and the occasion to influence the way you feel about food. In the sunshine, on the beach, I feel free of my usual agonising over doing the fish justice.

I watch the old men fish a little in the morning, play dominoes in the bar on the beach in the afternoon, eating simple food, and looking so happy with life. Would I get bored? Possibly. Maybe I should try it. Come and see me in six months. There I'll be on the beach, playing dominoes: beard, golden tan, not a care in the world . . .

. . . The return flight gets into London late, there is footie on the TV. Takeaway Chinese. Crispy duck and pancakes – always the business – prawns with salt and chilli; sweet and sour chicken and egg-fried rice.

Thursday

My flat looks like I'm going to rob a bank: you know that scene when the gang lay out all the plans everywhere.

6 a.m.

Story has been open for eighteen months and I want to re-model the downstairs kitchens. If you ever start to feel safe you're not doing enough. It is all about evolving, pushing harder and harder: myself, my team, the restaurant . . .

Everything is about 'now'. Everything is coming at me at a million miles an hour and I embrace that. When we were building Story, almost the last thing I thought about was the food. I felt I had trained my whole life for that.

It was all about, what are people going to see and feel when they walk through my door?

What do I want the atmosphere to be like?

Do I want it to be noisy and bustling?

How is the narrative of the food going to translate into the dining room?

What are the chairs we choose going to feel like after you have sat on them for a couple of hours?

How much space do I want around each table?

However far I felt I could push the food on the plate in terms of technique and approach, I wanted everything else to be as if you were eating at home, so that people could relax and have fun.

I don't put a tablecloth on my table at home to eat dinner, so I never wanted cloths in my restaurant.

Keep progressing; never stand still.

In eighteen months Story has become a snake that has outgrown its skin, so we need to shed it and start over. The food has grown, the team has grown, not only in numbers, but in standard. The environment we work in has to follow suit and acting now is a necessity.

I want to be more slick, more efficient. The lesson I learned way back in Tom Aikens's kitchen was that I never wanted my chefs to be in a situation where they had to fight over pans or trays or utensils.

I want to push the food further, invest in the bakery and pastry, and that means big changes and big costs. We need a second convection oven, so we can have one dedicated to baking breads, roasting bones for stocks, the other for steaming, or drying and dehydrating over night. A second oven alone is a £20,000 investment.

More capital, more risk, but in order to succeed, you have to be prepared to fail.

If we are going to continue on our journey I know this change is vital, but people think I am crazy.

I talk about ideas for two hours with FG, Angelo and Rod, the man who built our kitchens.

I've known Rod for ten years and he is a huge support. He tells a funny story about the first time we spoke when I was at Trinity. He was working for one of the big kitchen suppliers at the time and his sales manager told him he would have to take a call from a customer who was being 'very difficult'. I don't even remember the conversation, but apparently I wanted twenty copper pans and I wasn't happy with the deal they were offering, so the conversation went along the lines of:

— You know who this is? Tom Sellers. Do you know who I am?

— Sorry, I'm not sure I do.

— Well, you will do. Look after me now and I'll be calling you to look after my own kitchens.

It was all bravado, but all those years on here we are. Rod is the one who will turn my plans into substance, but the input from FG and Angelo is crucial too.

This isn't just about me; it's about the team. I am building a kitchen for all of us.

If I stopped every time someone said, 'You can't do that,' or 'You're crazy,' I would still be washing pots.

Monday

I wake up to twenty-nine emails. One of them is
from a company developing a new project in
Manhattan. 'Would you like to open a restaurant in
New York City?'   *10 a.m.*

Why not.

Today is our third major planning meeting for the
new downstairs kitchen at Story.

Building – or re-building – a restaurant kitchen is a
complex business.

Inevitably we will go through about twenty drafts
before everyone is happy, and there will be endless
debates with Rod and his team, that run along the
lines of:

  – We can probably do . . .

  – No, 'we will'.

It's all about parting the curtain between the
working part of the restaurant and the stage a little
more. So we're putting a glass panel along the side
of the downstairs kitchen that will allow guests to
see in.

We're talking about hundreds of thousands of
pounds, so every decision is crucial. We have one
shot at getting it right, maximising the space and

learning from the annoying malfunctions of some of the equipment in the glass box upstairs.

– No more sliding doors that wobble and bang and fall off, Rod!

– Probably because they get kicked, Tom.

– No, no, my boys don't kick doors.

Angelo has drawn his dream kitchen all over Rod's plans. He wants a glass panel around the porter's section, and a built-in Asian-style water bath: a digital bain-marie, 'super-precise'. A glass-fronted dairy fridge.

– Neon lit, wi-fi. Can you do that, Rod? Seriously why can't you? Come on, how long before fridges are wireless, in the world we live in? Can you imagine turning down the fridge by remote on your iPhone on your day off?

The next two hours are all about resins and concrete plinths, drainage, waste and water, cupboards, worktops, upgrades in electricity and walk-in cold rooms.

It's all about the detail: the right height of shelves and benches – higher than normal because we want everything on concrete plinths so nothing has to be cleaned underneath.

– Shall we tell Rod about our oil unit, Angelo? OK, we want you to build two tall, nine-litre cylinders, fitted into a metal frame, like Coke and Pepsi dispensers, and we're going to fill one with rapeseed oil and one with vegetable oil.

– Yeah, you just want some dispensers?

– Don't say, 'just', we're creating dreams here! Next chef's kitchen you build, you're going to say, 'I've got this great idea, two tall oil dispensers . . .'

— We will deliver your dreams, Tom!

In the dining room, we are replacing the old tables with new more sturdy, solid oak ones. Jon, the restaurant manager, is pouring red wine onto a sample table, and brushing it in with a toothbrush, to make sure the wood won't stain. We will have new racks for the house wines next to the bar, and a wine station for decanting older vintages.

When we opened Story I didn't envisage how much the noises of a busy bustling restaurant and kitchen would echo and bounce off the hard surfaces, so panels are being fitted on the ceiling and along one wall to help absorb and soften the sounds.

Scoob comes up from the downstairs kitchen where the contractors have adjourned to take measurements. 'One of them wanted to know if we had any microwaves. I told him no,' says Scoob. 'Then the guy said, "Well, do you plan to have any?" I said no again.' Scoob sounds quite incensed. 'What I really wanted to ask him was, "Do we look like the kind of restaurant that would have microwaves?" but I was too polite!'

'I'm Tom's emergency drinking partner. Text code: Woolpack. That means it's important; he needs to chat. I think of him as a bit like a pocket general. He has a very real, clear way of communicating that makes people pay attention. The first time I ate his food was at Trinity, when he was in charge of the kitchen. He came out and said, 'Are you guys ready? Seatbelts on.' It was one of the best meals I ever had. So when he told me about Story, I said, 'I'll do your menu design, your website, whatever you need for free'. I just wanted to help him succeed.'

David Ball,
BrandFuel

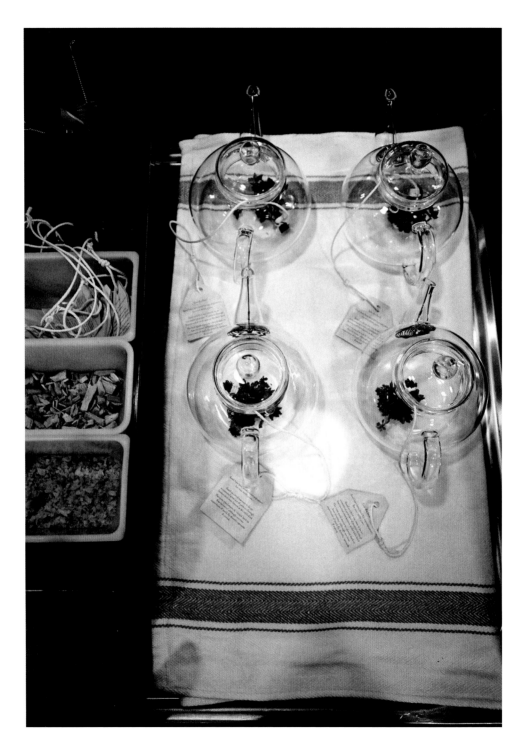

Service

Frank and Alice, 'the showbirds', are doing the rounds of the restaurant. Two quail, feathers still on, nestling in a basket of straw, with a handful of quail eggs. I'm watching the reaction of the guests as they are shown the basket and the waiting staff explain our new dish, tale of a quail.

Table 5 is in the house . . . but it is missing one person. It is 9 p.m. The guest arrives at 9.25 p.m., then goes out and takes a phone call. Forty minutes later we begin to send the first snacks to their table.

I step in to help, otherwise the boys will all have an hour's less sleep tonight.

TALE of a QUAIL

It's known as the Bible Bird, sent by God to feed the hungry.

A year-round bird, bred for our enjoyment for over four thousand years.

It's a dish of several servings.

For a small bird, the quail packs a lot of impact. Every part of it is used.

I love this dish because it involves a high level of craft and a combination of quite different thought and cooking processes.

As Angelo says, 'It's what we do: super-simple, but technically quite complex. It's the ultimate ingredient commitment: the lengths we go to to use every part of one small bird.'

You want the quail to shine, first, then you look at things like acidity, texture, and umami.

First we serve the quail and heather tea: essentially a consommé made with the carcass, served in a glass teapot, with a small crouton topped with quail liver parfait and truffle.

Next quail's eggs, which we smoke in the kitchen inside kilner jars in a basket of hay with little skewers of liver, heart and a piece of thigh, grilled on the barbeque. The legs are roasted, braised, de-boned, ballotined and glazed and served alongside the kebab.

The final serving is the breast, roasted on the crown, with corn pudding. You juice the corn, put it into a pan and whisk it as it heats. Because of the natural starches it releases, it thickens like custard. It is such an amazing thing, extraordinarily intense in flavour.

Next to it on the plate we have corn kernels, folded through with parsley stems, mustard seeds, shallots and a bit of umami action from a home-made soy, made with fermented mushrooms and barley, which we also brush onto the kebabs before they go under the grill.

Wednesday

We've been filming for a TV series, with a young kid who works in his mother's tea shop and wants to be a chef.

8 a.m.

We were picking green elderberries in the kitchen, cameras rolling, when he suddenly turned to me.

   — Can I say something? I think you are a knobhead. Is this all you do? Do you have a hobby? Do you even have a girlfriend? Do you just cook?

Well, yes to all of your questions, actually.

I tried to explain that here we strive for perfection every day.

   — See, that's disappointed me about you.

   — Sorry?

   — That you're striving for it.

   — Well, yes, because I don't think perfection exists, but we try to get as close as we possibly can.

I reckon he's thinking, 'I wanted a perfect Michelin-starred chef and I've got one that is only striving!'

'May the best of your yesterdays be the worst of your tomorrows.'
A great sentiment. It's an old Irish toast. You see people thinking about it for a moment, and then going, 'Yeah, I like that . . .'

Wild Stems

In the height of winter Miles came into the kitchen with a basket of stems. 'Look Tom, we have an abundance of these and no one is using them.'

Stems of thistle, sea radish, wild cabbage, water celery and hogweed.

He chopped them up in the kitchen and bound them in a little rapeseed oil, vinegar and salt, almost like a kind of coleslaw.

We fell in love with the idea of a dishful of vitamins and minerals that we could keep on the menu for twelve months of the year, passing through an entire cycle of stems gathered from the wild.

That isn't as easy as it sounds, because each stem has its own flavour profile and characteristics; some are quite hardy and fibrous and need to be blanched, others lose their flavour the moment that heat is applied, and it takes experimentation to find out the most respectful way to treat each one.

It's all about the stems, but there needs to be a protein, for texture as much as flavour.

Meat feels too robust. Where Miles forages, many of the plants grow along or near the shore; some are fed by the sea, some have a salty element, so my brain tells me to pair them with seafood.

So in winter we add creamy-textured raw squid, scored really finely in criss-crosses on both sides to tenderise it, then sliced in thin strips, and laid through the stems.

Then we make an earthy mushroom broth – many different varieties of mushroom, poached in water until all the flavour of them is infused into it – finished with a little soy for umami and to give a little body, and poured over the stems and squid at the table.

As the stems change through spring and summer, some flowering, some becoming lighter in flavour, we make a correspondingly lighter clam broth, and instead of squid, we serve the stems with langoustines, cut in half and warmed, shell-side down, in a pan of foaming butter.

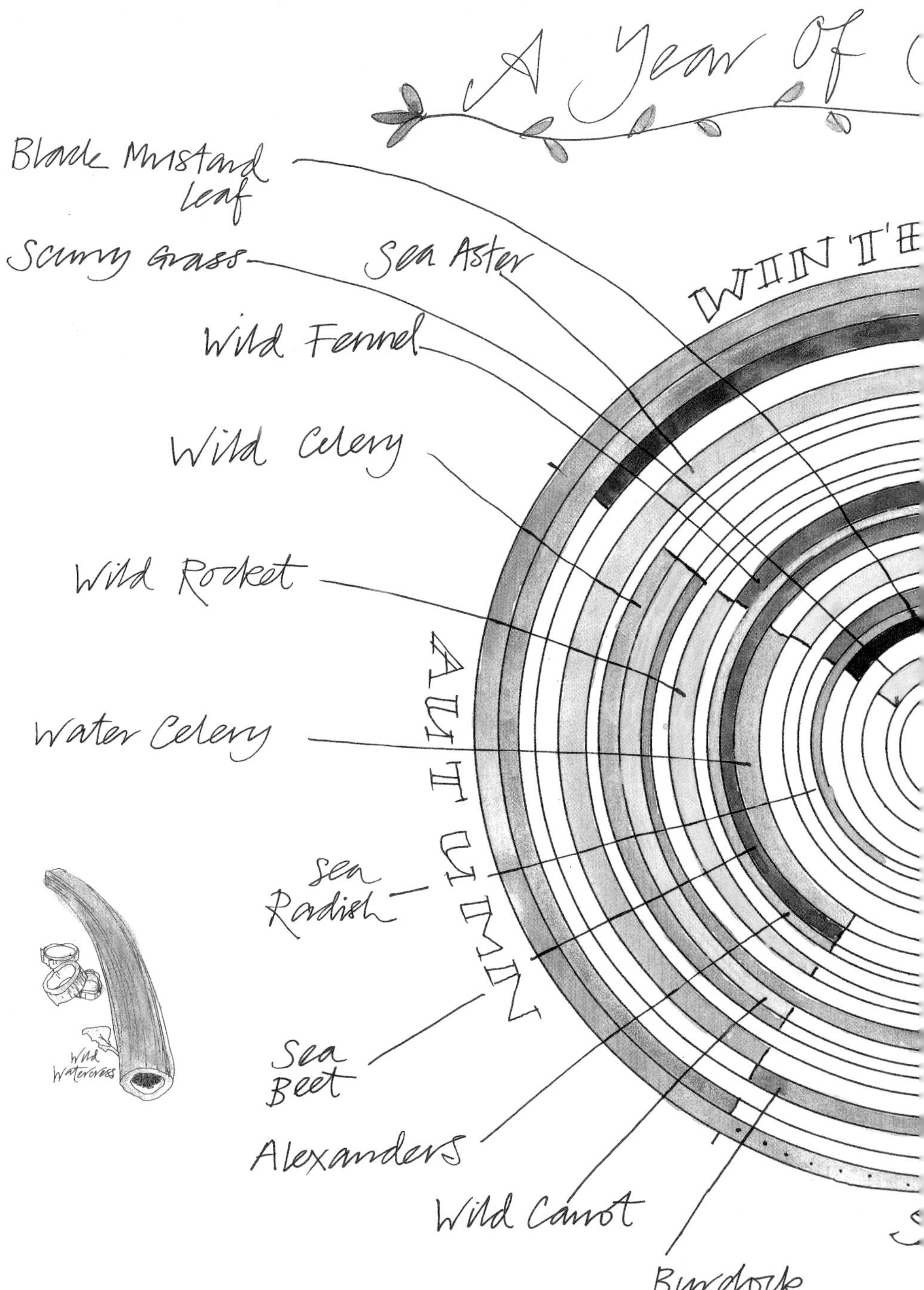

A Year of C

WINTE

Black Mustard Leaf

Scurvy Grass

Sea Aster

Wild Fennel

Wild Celery

Wild Rocket

Water Celery

AUTUMN

Sea Radish

Wild Watercress

Sea Beet

Alexanders

Wild Carrot

Burdock

S

alks + Stems

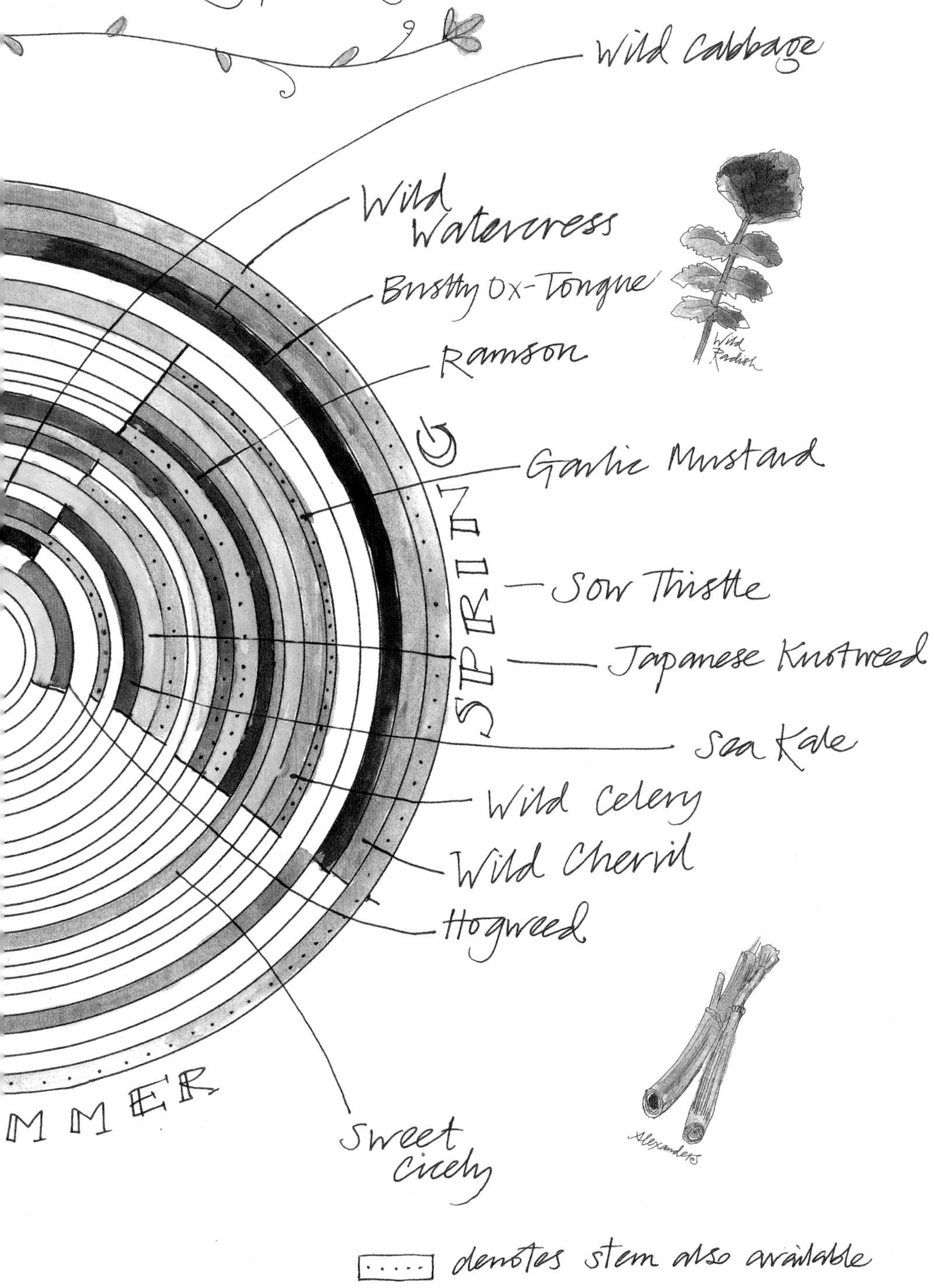

Wild Cabbage

Wild Watercress

Bristly Ox-Tongue

Wild Radish

Ramson

Garlic Mustard

SPRING

Sow Thistle

Japanese Knotweed

Sea Kale

Wild Celery

Wild Chervil

Hogweed

MMER

Sweet Cicely

Alexanders

[.....] denotes stem also available

Friday

My restaurant re-opens on Tuesday for dinner and it looks like a building site.

The contractors are still tiling and painting, and that is just downstairs. The dining room, where we have added a new wine station and a rack around the bar for the bottles of house wine, is under a layer of dust. They are telling me that they are on schedule and I couldn't have two better teams on it. If anyone can do it they can. But it is so tight.

4 p.m.

Irrationally perhaps, we are putting a brand new main course on for Tuesday night: fallow deer with cauliflower and yeast, dandelion and wild elderberry.

Angelo and I will have twenty-four hours to develop it from our drawings, notes and conversations.

We have been thinking about it for weeks because summer is almost gone and the season for lamb is over. The lamb dish that started out with a stutter has been purring along and it's a hard act to follow, but I am excited for next year, when the lamb will come back and we will tweak the dish and make it even better.

Soon the leaves will be falling, and so our cooking is turning autumnal. Bigger, bolder, richer, earthier, comforting flavours here and there. I love that rhythm of the kitchen that means we move seamlessly from season to season without skipping a beat.

The tale of a quail will be done with turnip and damson. The potato dish will be with radish; the foie gras brulée with apple, blackberry and cobnut.

The venison comes from young fallow deer from the Lake District, essentially wild, but so tame, they are almost farmed. A bigger, wilder red deer that forages and feeds for itself will be more muscular, and its meat more dense and inconsistent in texture, but the fallow deer are smaller, fed on grassland, sometimes even given food by visitors to the Lakes so their meat is tender, not gamey at all, almost like a cross between venison and lamb.

As has become our way, we are going to bring in the whole animal: serve the loin medium rare; braise the shoulder for a little pastilla; mince the rump and fat for a faggot; confit the belly and serve it crispy with a purée of cauliflower and yeast.

I love the whole idea of yeast because it represents growth, but for the cauliflower purée, we use it for its flavour, almost as a seasoning. We crumble in the fresh yeast when we cook the cauliflower and it activates, fizzes slightly, then when we blend the cauliflower the yeast gives it a rich, fermented character. Umami is the only way I can describe it.

Then we make a little savoury granola – I imagine it as a handful of grains that you might hold out in your hand to feed the deer: puffed rice, black rice, barley and malt extract. Dandelion stems, cooked in a little butter and chicken stock, the leaves chopped in at the last moment, for bitterness, and finally, the unifying blanket of love: venison sauce, split out with the reduced-down juice of red cabbage with butter montéed into it, finished with wild elderberries and wild elderberry vinegar.

For me it is a perfect example of cooking for the moment, the mood, the weather, the romance of the deer and the emotion that autumn brings.

Tuesday

The team in the downstairs kitchen are as happy as kids in a new playground.

The first batches of sourdough for the day are cooling, *10 a.m.* made as always from the starter, or 'mother' we have kept going for a year. Created originally from a ferment of flour, water, black treacle and grated Granny Smith apples.

Jack, who has found his vocation as a baker, is dividing buttermilk dough into little tins ready for baking and serving with cheese.

The baked wild fig dough for the cheese crisps is already in the freezer firming up, so that it can be thinly sliced and crisped in the oven. Next up is our new brioche loaf.

In the pastry section, the chocolate cloak is being poured over the dessert snack of rose marshmallow and raspberry purée teacakes.

Pieces of cod skin – ten from a fish – are steamed, pressed and dried. Quail eggs are being peeled, potato flesh scooped from skins.

After two weeks Restaurant Story has re-opened its doors. Yesterday, the moment the builders left, the entire front of house staff rolled up their sleeves and got down to cleaning and polishing.

We have two new snacks:

A layered egg roll that Angelo brought to the table. The technique for making it is supposed to resemble the traditional folding and laminating of steel in a Samurai sword. You make a wafer-thin omelette, then roll and fold it over and over on itself into a log shape, and move it to one end of the pan. Pour in some more egg, let it begin to set, then roll your log back over it. Keep repeating that, backwards and forwards, until you have fine layer after fine layer of omelette. We slice it and make it relevant to our British story with a garnish of English caviar and chives.

And SOS: snacks of the sea. A collection of our seafood favourites and some new ones, arranged in a big basket of stones.

Scallop tartare with diced raw scallop, crème fraîche and sheets of apple jelly, sitting in a scallop shell.

Devilled crab inside a hollowed-out crab claw.

Razor clams with champagne and barley, fried so it puffs up, and champagne snow.

Wild shrimp – they come from the ocean to us in less than six hours, still live and kicking. We take off the central section of shell and deep fry the head at one end and tail at the other, until crispy, leaving the rawness in between to give a contrast of textures. Then we dress them with rapeseed oil and salt.

And nasturtiums filled with oyster emulsion. The emulsion just made from oysters, parsley and oil, no egg. There is enough protein in an oyster to create an emulsion, but it requires a lot of skill. We had many failed attempts, before we understood that temperature was the key. In the back of my mind

I remembered the lesson I learned as a young chef, trying to keep a mayonnaise from splitting in a blender that was still warm from the dishwasher.

First we started putting the oil in the freezer to chill it, then we put in the whole blender. Once everything is super-cold then the emulsion will hold together.

Angelo or FG will bring the basket to the table, explain all the elements and then pour liquid nitrogen into a bowl of hot sea water to create a cloud of vapour, for a bit of theatre.

I'm playing around in my head with a dish called goose fair, prompted by the Nottingham Goose Fair which has been held every October for over seven hundred years. Our whole family would go every year when I was growing up. I don't know yet what I am going to do with it, but I know there will be brandy in there, because my dad would always buy brandy snaps from one of the stalls.

At 11.45 a.m. Angelo takes the kitchen briefing; Jon briefs the floor staff.

The guy on Table 5 has rung Lindsay to warn us that he is intending to propose to his girlfriend over lunch. It happens every now and then; makes the service a little more interesting. Everyone has to stay alert. Imagine presenting the show quails, Frank and Alice, at the crucial moment.

Friday

A key member of our team, Simon has handed in his notice, and the timing couldn't be worse.

It's hard to take, because he figured highly in my plans.   *10 a.m.*

The reality is that the best are always going to be hard to hang onto. Young, talented, driven chefs are always going to be hungry for new challenges, different experiences. I see myself in them, and I respect that there will come a time when they will need to move on.

You can't hold someone back, but you want to see them move for the right reasons.

If the only attraction is more money, than I feel frustrated. For me and for them. Because every decision you make can affect your entire career path. Simon was going for the right reasons, but as always, when a chef leaves, I question what I could have done to prevent it from happening.

What did I do wrong?

Should I have seen it coming? Pre-empted it in some way?

Ultimately it isn't only me it affects, but the whole team.

Simon will go with one hundred per cent praise; he has been a fantastic asset to Story. I don't have a bad word to say about him.

But what hurts is that he didn't come to talk to me before making a decision.

Could I have changed his mind? I don't know. But I would have liked to try.

Everyone is replaceable, in theory, but there are people you don't want to replace.

I'm reminded, as I have been many, many times since opening the restaurant, that however important people become to you, whatever emotional bond you build, you have to try to keep some professional detachment.

They come, they go. 'And the wheels on the bus go round and round . . .'

CLEMENTINE

There are very few desserts that make me totally happy. Almond and dill is one. The new clementine dish is another: burnt clementine consommé, smoked rapeseed oil, pumpkin, carrot and cardamom. It's a massively seasonal, festive dish, but without doubt it will come back again. When we make it the kitchen is filled with that burnt toffee orange smell that reminds me of Christmas. I'm thinking of Rudolph eating carrots when he delivers the presents, and all those deep-spicy flavours that go into puddings and mulled wine.

We peel the clementines and then blacken them on the Green Egg, pulp the flesh then hang it in cheesecloth to filter the clear, dark orange liquid for the consommé, which for me is the stand-out element of the dessert, the cloak that I always look for, that brings together all the elements.

We take fresh slices of pumpkin and lightly pickle them in vinegar, sugar and water, make a pumpkin ice cream, and a tuile from puréed pumpkin mixed with glucose, spread out into a wafer-thin almost transparent sheet and put into a cool oven until it crisps.

Carrot and pumpkin naturally go together, I believe. We overcook the carrots, slice them, then dry them almost like raisins, so their natural sugars concentrate, their flavour intensifies and they become slightly chewy, like little orange rosette-shaped sweets.

With a dish like this you have to present it in a way that means that the guest experiences all the flavours together, so we serve it in a bowl, starting with some English crème fraîche, which provides the body and fat of the dish. Then fresh segments of clementine to balance out the burnt consommé which surrounds everything, purple and green lemony-tasting sheep's sorrel for acidity, toasted pumpkin seeds, and spicy, medicinal cardamom. The pumpkin tuile goes on top, so you crack through it and scoop up a mouthful of everything underneath: perfumey, deep and spicy; charred, but fresh all at the same time.

New Year

It is time to re-focus on the whole Story experience: our identity. Never rest on your laurels; make those small but important tweaks in the dining room, in the kitchen, in the office; find another level, and then another level, and another. When you are trying to develop a business, it can be so easy to take your eye off the goal. We have to remind ourselves of what is important: to be able to look at ourselves in the mirror and know we have done everything we can to be better every day.

I want to grow the office by four people in the next few weeks. We need to be more efficient. I can see that each week we are missing between two and three hundred phone calls from people who can't get through. Of those, only around half will leave a voicemail and a number to call them back on. And by the time we speak to them, another half will have booked somewhere else, or we can't meet their requirements. We need to talk to every single person to explain that being on a waiting list is a good thing, because there is every possibility of a cancellation.

And I'm looking at a site across the road for a new research and development kitchen, private rooms, staff quarters; somewhere our lunchtime guests can have their digestives and coffee. I like the idea of a waiter taking them over so they can extend the experience by looking into the development kitchen, asking questions, relaxing for as long as they like. The first new main course of the year is veal, rhubarb and roots. We all loved the deer main course, but I wanted to move on. My mind jumps from one thing to the next constantly. I can't rest. We need to continually challenge ourselves.

The winter is a tough time of year for a seasonal cook. At first you are excited about all the things you can do with root vegetables, but by January/February the time starts to drag and you feel like you've been eating turnip and swede for months. You can't wait for the first shoots of spring, and then the first shocking pink rhubarb comes in from the forcing sheds in Yorkshire, where they bring the stems on in the pitch darkness.

The obvious thing to do is to put the rhubarb into a dessert, but I wanted to use it in a savoury way. So we lightly pickle it in grenadine with a tiny touch of sugar, so it stays quite tart; and serve it with veal, a lighter meat than deer.

The story is the transition from winter to spring that you know is coming, but isn't quite there yet. I wanted the dish to sum up those cold January days when it is icy cold out, but the sun is shining, and you feel hopeful and happy.

So we are still using some roots, in this case Jerusalem artichoke, baked in white wine, chicken stock, thyme and peppercorns and finished with a lemon brioche crust; along with leeks, blanched and barbecued on the Green Egg, and their roots deep-fried. But we are also adding wild young stems of watercress, celery, chervil.

We confit the veal belly and roast the loin, braise the sweetbreads in Noilly Prat and reduce the liquid down with squid ink to make a black sauce, some of which we use to glaze the sweetbreads so they look like stones. Veal sweetbreads are one of my favourite things in the world. Ask most chefs and they will tell you they love cooking them, love eating them. It's hard to say why exactly, it's everything about them: the flavour, the texture.

The way we plate the dish is to dust the sweetbreads in a powder made from burnt onions, to represent the blackness of the earth, with the roots and leeks and the bright rhubarb coming through, and the small stems on top – the growth towards spring – with the rest of the squid ink sauce, split with rapeseed oil, drawing the whole dish together.

BREAD & BUTTER

For a long time I wanted to introduce a second serving of bread to the menu. The bread and dripping candle will always be there but it is so personal, so linked to my relationship with my father and working-class England, that I wanted to revisit bread further through the courses in a different, special way.

Angelo and I had talked for a long time about putting one dish on the menu that projected craftsmanship, beauty and elegance. I've always said that I don't like to manipulate food, and that is true. Of course all of our dishes involve an element of craftsmanship but the focus is on the nature of the produce and everything stems from that. But I have always felt that there is something really attractive about presenting a single Rubik's cube of a dish that when it comes to the table is a bit of a puzzle, but you can appreciate the extraordinary amount of time and expertise that has gone into achieving it.

Our second serving of bread – and butter – ticks both boxes. In all honesty the credit should go to Angelo, because after one of our long conversations about craftsmanship, he said, 'I have an idea.'

 – *OK. Let's look at it.*

It isn't often that I am lost for words, but when he put it in front of me, it was one of those moments. It just made me smile from ear to ear.

First there is a little layer cake of butter, truffle, foie gras and parsley. We punch discs of butter from sheets that have been rolled and then flattened between two layers of Perspex, then punch a smaller disc from the centre of each one, to make doughnut-like rings of butter. We fill the centre of each one with alternate thin discs of truffle, foie gras and parsley then another disc of butter, the size of the original ones, goes over the top and is gently blow torched so that it melts around like icing. When the 'cake' is set and cut in half, vertically, you can see all the layers inside.

Alongside it is a 'terrine' of butter. We take whole cucumbers that have been pickled with parsley stems and shallots, then cut them lengthways into long batons and insert them into good butter, which we roll like a fat sausage, chill and slice into rounds, so that each disk is studded with pieces of cucumber. I love the look of them, they remind me of a cobblestone path.

Then, the bread: an individual, light brioche, made to a recipe we worked on for a long time and which is baked to order and served warm.

It's a dish that is special to me, because it showed me, yet again, how blessed I am to have great, talented people like Angelo working with me. You don't always succeed at the things you aspire to, but in this case we wanted to create something beautiful and craft-led and we achieved it. I think it will be part of the menu forever.

Tuesday

We are celebrating the pig. There's nothing new about cooking with every part of it, of course. Everywhere I have worked I have seen great things done with it, from Tom's spiced pig's head to Adam Byatt's trotters.

7 a.m.

So it's a dish that pays homage to many influences, but served in two parts in a way that is totally our own. First a condiment tray: a teapot filled with a broth of smoked ham hock which you pour over a piece of pork belly, served with dehydrated kale; pork belly barbecued on the Green Egg with miso and soy; deep-fried pig's trotter fingers with sauce gribiche; home-made black pudding served with apple; and dried and fried crispy pork skin.

Then we send out a classic braised pig's head torchon, inspired by a dish we did at Per Se. The heads are braised, then the meat pulled out and rolled up like a ballotine, wrapped in a cheesecloth and then put back into the braising liquor to sit and set. We slice it and serve it with pickles and salad, which you eat with bread crisps – thinly sliced bread dried in the oven.

I like it. But is it definitive enough to stay on the menu for long? I don't know. I'm a tough one to please.

There is a buzz about the floor and the kitchen. I am surrounded by talented people who believe in what we are building, who come in on their days off to discuss new ideas, initiatives. It makes me proud.

As always things are moving on in my head very fast. The veal dish has been on the menu for three weeks now. Everyone in the kitchen and the dining room loves it but I can't give myself full marks for it. The craftsmanship isn't enough. I think we can do better. We will go back to the beginning and start over with a new animal.

Some days I feel like I have so many ideas, I am only just getting started.

TOMATO & VANILLA

The food memory bank is an incredibly powerful thing. During my short, jaded time at Troisgros in France one of my first jobs was to clean the walk-in fridge. Inside was a massive container of small red balls submerged in liquid, which turned out to be peeled and blanched tomatoes in a stock syrup made with loads of vanilla. I shouldn't have touched them, but I wanted to know what they tasted like, so I took a tomato and ate it. And it blew my mind. The combination of tomato and vanilla flavours was just awesome.

I never found out how they were used in the restaurant, and I never consciously thought about that moment again until, fast forward a few years, I am standing in the kitchen at Story with a box of beautiful Isle of Wight tomatoes, thinking, 'What are we going to do with these?' and vanilla jumps back into my head.

So we made a consommé with tomatoes, onion, garlic, basil, and lots of vanilla pods, a little bit of vinegar, salt and sugar, let it macerate for three days, spun it and hung it through muslin to get a clear liquid. Then we scraped more fresh vanilla seeds into it. We simply sliced the brilliant tomatoes, dressed them with the tomato and vanilla consommé, and served them with some vanilla salt, and buttermilk bread, lightly fried and air dried, almost like a play on panzanella. That was it. Done. The moment I tasted the dish I knew we didn't need to do anything more to it. Sometimes food just feels that simple.

It's strange and funny to think that from a single experience of eating something I shouldn't have, in the kitchen of a famous restaurant where I counted my time as a failure, I now have an inspired dish on my menu which pays homage to the Restaurant Troisgros. Everything I believe about the power of food and memory is summed up in that dish.

Sunday

So much has been happening, I need to take time out and catch up with Angelo.

We go out for something to eat, discuss the new menu, where we will take it to next, and make a promise that together we will drive this restaurant to where we think it deserves to be.

Then he asks a poignant question.

   – Chef, do you ever find it difficult to live like this?

   – What do you mean?

   – The constant striving for perfection. Sometimes it feels like one of the most harmful things to the mind and soul. Whatever we do, we always think we can do it better. Doesn't it beat you up inside?

What can I tell him, other than that to hear him ask that, I know I have the right person alongside me.

Because I have the same demons; the same conversation in my head.

It's a conversation that will go on forever. There is no finishing line.

I can't imagine the time when I will go home and think, 'That was a truly great day. I wouldn't change a thing.'

Sometimes, I envy the man that is happy with OK.

But what is happiness anyway? Or perfection?

A pursuit. Nothing more.

About Tom

It takes a certain kind of person to have the self-assurance to cast aside the stifling burden of worry that most of us carry about – how we are perceived by others; whether we are liked or not. Tom Sellers is that person. And I think it is one of his greatest attributes. He is truly genuine, honest, and never anything other than himself. Being less concerned about what people think gives him a positive energy that is infectious. I think it's the reason he is successful, respected and loved by those who know him well. I can confidently say that he's among the best of the 'good people' I know; but he will be the first to tell you his self-assurance can easily be misinterpreted. Especially when you meet him for the first time. I know. I didn't warm to him at all when we first met on a photoshoot back in 2013.

Will Poulter,
Actor

I had heard of Restaurant Story and I knew a rock-and-roll reputation preceded Tom Sellers. But that was all I knew.

– I'm Tom. Nice to meet you. You're an actor.

– Nice to meet you too, man. You're a chef. I've heard great things about your restaurant.

– Yeah . . . one Michelin star at twenty-six. Not bad for a kid from a rough part of Nottingham.

I just thought he was arrogant. But as the day went on we talked more. Neither of us felt particularly comfortable on the photoshoot, surrounded by much more photogenic people, and I was glad I wasn't the only one who felt out of place. The more time I spent in his company the more he struck me as a grounded professional who was just trying to come to terms with the hysteria and unrelenting pressure that had recently taken over his world. He made me totally re-evaluate his first words, which I had taken to be shameless self-promotion. I realised that all Tom was saying was: 'This is who I am, take it or leave it.' A common love for food and film, a shared sense of humour and the fact that we were both young, in turbulent, high-pressure industries, meant we related to each other. We hung out a few times after that and become friends very quickly.

Tom is great company but I know he's not always easy to work for. He demands the highest of standards and he doesn't mince words. I've witnessed him on the phone in work-related conversations being very direct, aggressive sometimes. I imagine it pisses a lot of people off. But as a friend he is thoughtful, loyal, exceptionally generous with his time and he has a fantastic sense of humour.

I witnessed both sides of his personality in the space of a few minutes when he invited me to come and cook with him one day. Story is closed on a Monday, but Tom was going in on his day off to prepare a week's worth of healthy, immune-system-boosting meals to package up and send to a friend who had become very ill. Did I want to be his impromptu sous chef? The circumstances were less than happy but the mood was light-hearted. We had a beer, put on some music, and had fun. Even though he wasn't cooking for a restaurant full of customers there was no way Tom was going to relax his attention to detail and allow me to mess things up, so I was given supposedly foolproof jobs like shelling peas and sorting different leaves to put into ice baths. The last task was to remove the seeds from a bowl of pomegranates, a

pain-in-the-arse of a job really, involving a lot of bang-
ing with the back of a spoon and inevitably getting pith
all mixed up with the seeds, but I was enjoying myself,
trying to show I could keep up with Tom's pace while
we chatted away. Suddenly he stopped mid-sentence. It
was as if he was physically frozen with anger. Then he
blinked and I realised that I had flicked a pomegranate
seed into his eye. 'Sorry . . .' I ventured gingerly. In a split
second he had changed from easygoing, funny, friendly
Tom. I didn't honestly think he was going to hurl a pan
at me or throw me out of the kitchen, and he defused
instantly, but just for an instant I had glimpsed his
potential for anger. Since then he's told me any number
of stories of craziness and flashpoints in kitchens. 'I used
to be nuts,' he tells me. And I believe it.

We work in totally different industries and come from
very different worlds, but I have huge admiration for
Tom's approach to life. His motto is pretty much that
if you want anything badly enough and you work hard
enough to achieve it, it can be yours. He has a more
flowery version of that message inked into his skin!

Ambition is one thing, work ethic is another and you need
both to be successful; but there is a third very important
but less acknowledged ingredient: resilience. It's the thing
that makes you continue to pursue the wildest of ambi-
tions, regardless of anything put before you, and it is the
thing that will help you to prosper in the end. I believe
that Tom is destined for happiness and success because he
is at ease with who he is and his self-assurance means he
is no obstacle to himself. If I've learned one thing from
Tom Sellers, other than how not to de-seed a pomegranate,
it's that you should never stop believing in yourself.

Thank You.